C0-AXC-269

FREEDOM OF THE HIGH SCHOOL PRESS

Nicholas D. Kristof

UNIVERSITY
PRESS OF
AMERICA

LANHAM • NEW YORK • LONDON

157159

Copyright © 1983 by

University Press of America,™ Inc.

4720 Boston Way
Lanham, MD 20706

3 Henrietta Street
London WC2E 8LU England

All rights reserved

Printed in the United States of America

Library of Congress Cataloging in Publication Data

Kristof, Nicholas D., 1959-
    Freedom of the high school press.

    Bibliography: p.
    1. Student newspapers and periodicals—Censorship—
United States.   I. Title.
KF4775.K74   1983   323.44`5   83-14511
ISBN 0-8191-3433-3 (alk. paper)
ISBN 0-8191-3434-1 (pbk. : alk. paper)

Dedication

To all those students who have sought to strike the spark of freedom in their schools--for illumination and not just heat--and especially to the 1976-77 staff of the *Y-C Expression* at Yamhill-Carlton Union High School in Yamhill, Oregon.

Table of Contents

157159

Preface

   This book started as a senior thesis at Harvard
University, where it no doubt spurred the local economy
with the purchase of hundreds of note cards and gallons
of coffee. The survey reported in this book was
financed by a $490 grant from the Harvard Government
Department. Only later did I learn that the chairman of
the department thought when he approved the grant that
the money would come from other coffers. The Government
Department also generously provided a tremendous
amount of computer time--so much that in subsequent
years students were no longer permitted to write their
theses on the department's computers.

   My thesis advisor, Prof. H.N. Hirsch, was of great
help and encouragement throughout. Prof. Ethel Klein
kindly read Chapter II and made some very useful
suggestions for analyzing the survey results and
presenting the statistics. David E. Sanger, a fellow
student, read most of the manuscript and made many
useful suggestions. My parents, Ladis and Jane Kristof,
were supremely helpful--as they always are--in reading
and rereading the manuscript and in offering
encouragement.

   The Student Press Law Center in Washington, D.C.,
provided me with vast quantities of information, as did
the Center for Law and Education at Harvard University.
Many librarians, on both sides of the Atlantic, helped
me find what I was looking for in the bowels of law
libraries. Finally, countless friends helped in other
ways: suggesting references, finding bugs in computer
programs, or interrupting my work for a beer or a game
of football. Notwithstanding all this assistance, I am
acutely aware of the pitfalls of attempting an
inter-disciplinary study such as this one. While the
counsel acknowledged above has greatly improved the

manuscipt, I accept full responsibility for any remaining errors. I would be most grateful to have them pointed out, if any reader would send me comments or criticisms or suggestions.

Nicholas D. Kristof
Oxford, England
Dec. 6, 1982

Note on Legal Citations

Court cases cited in this book follow the standard form suggested in *A Uniform system of Citation*, 12th ed. (Cambridge, Mass.: Harvard Law Review Press Association, 1976). Following the name of the case, the volume number of the series and the page number are listed. For example, *Tinker v. Des Moines School District*, 393 U.S. 503 (1969), means that this case begins on page 503 of volume 393 of U.S. Reports, indicating that it is a Supreme Court case. The year is listed afterward in parentheses. Federal circuit cases are listed in the Federal Reporter, 2nd Series, which is abbreviated F.2d. Therefore, *Gambino v. Fairfax County School Board*, 564 F.2d 157 (4th Cir. 1977) means that *Gambino* was decided by the Fourth Circuit in 1977 and begins on page 157 of volume 564 of the Federal Reporter, 2nd Series.

U.S. District Court cases are reported in the Federal Supplement, with the state and district listed in parentheses at the end of the citation. For example, *Frasca v. Andrews*, 463 F. Supp. 1043 (E.D.N.Y. 1978), was decided in the eastern district of New York and begins on page 1043 of volume 463 of the Federal Supplement. Other abbreviations for serials include N.W. for Northwest; P.2d for Pacific Reporter, 2nd series; Cal. Rep. for California Reporter; and Med. L. Rep. for Media Law Reporter.

When a specific passage in a case is cited, the footnote lists the page it is from, with a comma to separate the page on which the case begins. For example, 411 U.S. 623, 627 means that the case begins on page 623 and that the passage to which the footnote refers is on page 627. If the footnote is to the same case as the previous footnote, only the volume number, series and specific page number are listed: 411 U.S. at

630. For clarity, the legal forms of citation are used only for cases and not for books or law review articles.

I
INTRODUCTION

An enormous gulf exists in the United States between rights of students and rights of adults. While Americans generally are tolerant of most of those with whom they disagree, this consensus for freedom of expression applies only to adult civilians. There is no agreement that students, soldiers or prisoners should be granted even the most basic rights of free press or free speech. Of these groups that society excludes from the blanket of free expression, the largest and most important is students. High school students usually are old enough by the time they graduate to vote, to hold political office or to go to war. Yet they frequently are forbidden to voice even mild criticism of school officials or policies. In civics classes they learn of America's heritage of freedom of expression, but in journalism classes they discover that this freedom rings hollow in the schools.

The issue of student rights is today at the cutting edge of the struggle for freedom of expression. The freedoms at issue are not in extreme or uncharted areas, but are fundamental liberties that, among adults, have been respected for the most part in the United States for nearly two centuries. Despite a multitude of court decisions in the last dozen years prohibiting most censorship in high school publications, no consensus has evolved that students should be permitted to write what they want, and censorship remains commonplace.

"Censorship," as used here, refers not only to specific incidents where controversial material is excised, but also to any official policy or atmosphere of intimidation that discourages students from

1

including certain articles or advertisements in the student newspaper. Like a copy editor at a commercial newspaper, an adviser may edit a reporter's story. However, at a high school newspaper as at a metropolitan daily, the final authority should be the editor. If the student editor objects to the editing, that objection should be final. The adviser may seek to convince the editor of the wisdom of the changes, but censorship occurs when the adviser seeks not only to convince but also to coerce.

It does not matter, at least with a high school paper, whether the material that is censored is political or even critical. In a school setting, the censor need not have "the purpose of protecting a preferred belief or attitude";[1] an adviser's insistence even upon certain rules of grammar could constitute censorship because the rules would interfere with the principle of student control of the publication. Censorship, therefore, may deal with matters of style as well as of substance, because, in the picayune as well as the political, censorship erodes the student editor's authority and subverts the student character of the publication. Accordingly, a satisfactory definition of censorship, for the purposes of this book, is any official interference by intimidation or coercion with student control of the newspaper.

This study will examine the issue of censorship from four perspectives, which will form the subsequent chapters of this book. Those four areas of analysis are as follows: (1) as an empirical matter, censorship is widespread and exists at the vast majority of public high schools, sparking innumerable conflicts and affecting most young people as either staff or readers of student newspapers; (2) the issue focuses on a sector of society that until recently was excluded from the protection of most constitutional rights, and thus raises certain interesting philosophical questions about the role of paternalism in a democratic society, (3) scores of court cases have dealt with student newspaper censorship, and a considerable case law has emerged; (4) because of the socializing role played

---

1. This ideological motive is stipulated as part of the definition of censorship offered by Benjamin C. Cox, "The Varieties of Censorial Experience: Toward a Definition of Censorship," *The High School Journal*, Vol. 62, No. 8 (May 1979), p. 313.

by the schools, the degree of freedom in high schools may shape adult attitudes and thus the degree of freedom in society.

Conflicts over censorship in student newspapers are a relatively new phenomenon, dating from the politicization and unrest among students during the 1960's. Before then, it was generally accepted that principals and advisers had the authority--and probably the obligation--to review material and excise the controversial. There was little of controversy, however, in the earliest student newspapers-- publications like the *Student's Gazette* of Penn Charter School in Philadelphia (begun in 1777 or earlier), *The Literary Journal* of Boston Latin School (1829) and the *Effort* in Hartford, Connecticut (1851).[2] Moreover, these newspapers were not produced under the auspices of the schools but were prepared by groups of students working in their own time without supervision.

High schools first offered classes in journalism in 1912, and it soon became standard for a high school to have a journalism class that produced a school newspaper.[3] With school support, student newspapers became more professional--in the sense that the writing was better and that they looked more like commercial newspapers. But they also became more like house public relations newsletters, with the expectation that they would propagandize for the school and cover only "good news." The result was a tension between increased professionalism, which implied aggressive, skeptical reporting, and the tendency of administrators to see the school newspaper as a public relations tool. This tension reached a breaking point in the 1960's, as the baby boom generation demanded student rights and protested the Vietnam War and civil rights violations.

The student unrest of the 1960's was by no means confined to colleges, for the *American School Board Journal* reported "more incidents of student unrest in the *high schools* than in the colleges."[4] Student

---

2. Edgar G. Johnston and Roland C. Faunce, *Student Activities in Secondary Schools* (New York: Ronald Press, 1952), p. 171.
3. *Teacher's Guide to High School Journalism* (Indianapolis: Indiana State Department of Public Instruction, Bulletin No. 501, 1965), p. vii.
4. Gregory R. Anrig, "Those High School Protestors: Can Boards Put Up With Much More?" *American School*

3

newspapers reflected the new turbulence in the high
schools. As editors rebelled against the policies of
the United States government, they also began to
question the policies of their schools. Finally, in
1969, the Supreme Court ruled that the First Amendment
does protect expression by high school students,[5] and
later cases established that under most circumstances
censorship at public high schools is unconstitutional.

A dozen years after censorship was declared
unconstitutional, it remains widespread, according to
the results of a survey conducted as part of the
research for this book.[6] More than 80 percent of
student editors either reported censorship or said they
would be censored if they wrote something
controversial. The survey found that while
administrators do not often actually forbid publication
of specific articles, teachers and administrators are
likely to discourage students from printing
controversial articles in general. This policy of
discouraging aggressive reporting is often backed by
implicit or explicit threats of discipline that result
in stifling self-censorship by the students themselves.

Another interesting finding of the survey is that
student editors at many schools are extremely
deferential toward school authorities. Many editors say
the school newspaper should focus primarily on positive
news, and when presented with hypothetical news events
that might cast the administration in a bad light, many
editors say they would not cover the events. Therefore,
a lack of conflict over censorship in a school is as
likely to indicate a deferential and submissive editor
as it is a tolerant principal.

This survey is significant because it is the first
reliable statistical study of censorship in secondary
schools. A half-dozen other surveys have been conducted
in the last decade, but they either were not national
in scope or suffered from poor sampling procedures. In
this survey, questionnaires were sent to student

Board Journal, Vol. 157, No. 4 (October 1969), p.
20 (emphasis in the original). For the results of a
survey of protests in high schools during the
1960's, see J. Lloyd Trump and Jane Hunt, "The
Nature and Extent of Student Activism," _NASSP
Bulletin_, Vol. 53 (May 1969), pp. 150-58.
5. Tinker v. Des Moines School District, 393 U.S. 503.
6. The survey was funded by a grant from the
Department of Government of Harvard University.

editors at 500 randomly selected public high schools in all 50 states and the District of Columbia. The response rate was more than 75 percent, and some schools that did not respond were telephoned to determine if their conditions were different from those at schools that returned the surveys.

Beyond the empirical issue is the normative question of how much freedom high school students should have. Essentially the question is one of freedom versus order. Those placing a premium on order, here termed conservatives, offer four principal arguments in support of restraining expression on high school campuses. Free speech, the argument runs, would lead to insubordination and would undermine respect for teachers to the point that students would learn less. Second, the conservatives argue that high school students are not yet mature enough to handle the responsibilities of publishing a newspaper. They say that students must be protected from themselves because they lack the wisdom and experience to wield the power of the press properly. Third, supporters of censorship insist that this is not an issue of rights but one of how to teach good journalism. In this light, the newspaper is seen not as a forum for expression but as a laboratory project for the teacher to use in journalism class. As in any other class, the teacher and the principal are the final authorities. Fourth and finally, the conservatives argue that censorship is a practical necessity to screen for libel and to prevent community outrage.

The liberal critique of these justifications grew from a new perspective on education. Partly due to the influence of John Dewey, students came to be seen in the 20th century as autonomous individuals deserving respect and rights. The liberals offer four counter-arguments to the conservatives. First, they say, it is rights, not authority and discipline, that prepare students for roles as citizens in a democracy. Moreover, free expression is a natural right that must be extended to all persons in a society, including students. Second, the liberals note that dangers are associated with the exercise of many rights, but that the potential for abuse is not seen as a sufficient reason to withhold a right or privilege. Third, liberals argue that a student newspaper is different from teaching tools used in other classes because the newspaper becomes a forum for ideas, and with ideas there is no clear right or wrong. Furthermore, if the newspaper is to be used to educate students, it can do

5

this best by demonstrating the role that disagreement and free expression play in a democracy. Finally, the liberal critique acknowledges that libel is a danger, but sees the solution in holding the students and the newspaper, and not the school, liable for damages. Nor is adverse community reaction a reason for controlling the newspaper, for the purpose of the fourth estate is to inform and persuade, not to please or pass the school budget.

Only in recent years have portions of the liberal critique been accepted by the courts. For most of the history of high school newspapers, courts declined to interfere with school policies toward student newspapers. Judges held that schools could punish students for criticizing school officials because of the need to cultivate obedience and respect for authority. Then in a landmark decision in 1969, *Tinker v. Des Moines School District,* the Supreme Court ruled that, "It can hardly be argued that either students or teachers shed their constitutional rights to freedom of speech or expression at the schoolhouse gate."[7]

Tinker deals specifically with symbolic expression--two high school students and one junior high student had been suspended for wearing black armbands to school to protest the Vietnam War--but subsequent cases in lower courts extended this holding to freedom of expression in student newspapers. The test used in *Tinker,* and afterward in censorship cases, was whether the expression would "materially and substantially interfere" with the educational process. If it would cause this disruption, the expression could be censored; otherwise it had to be tolerated. Different courts have interpreted this test in different ways, and there remain some glaring contradictions among the rulings. For example, it is not clear whether prior restraint is ever permissible, or whether student journalists have any right of access to the news. These complexities aside, the basic right of students to publish controversial articles and editorials is secure--at least in current legal theory.

This right is not secure in the real world, however, as the survey for this book shows. It is unclear whether growing up in an intolerant educational atmosphere will have any long-term impact upon the students, or whether as adults they will mimic the

7.   393 U.S. 503, 506.

authoritarianism and proclivity for order they encountered in the schools. Certainly high schools do play some role in socializing young people and shaping their attitudes about participation in a democracy. The degree of this socializing influence is unclear, and different studies disagree as to whether high school or elementary school is the crucial period for socialization.[8] Studies have shown that high school students are markedly intolerant of ideas with which they disagree, but no one has demonstrated a conclusive link between tolerant high schools and tolerant graduates.

The literature relating to student press rights for the most part discusses broader issues in which high school journalism plays a part. Almost all the literature dates from *Tinker*, and most focuses on the case law that has developed around the rights of high school and college students. The landmark study of free expression in high schools was commissioned by the Robert F. Kennedy Memorial and published in 1974 under the title *Captive Voices: High School Journalism in America*. The report, which called for complete student control of school newspapers, found that

> censorship and the systematic lack of freedom to engage in open, responsible journalism characterize high school journalism. Unconstitutional and arbitrary restraints are so deeply embedded in high school journalism as to over-shadow its achievements, as well as its other problems.[9]

Captive Voices also found a pervasive self-censorship, because of fear of punishment and unpleasantness, that "has created passivity among students and made them cynical about the guarantees of a free press under the First Amendment."[10] The report concluded:

> Censorship is the fundamental cause of the trivi-ality, innocuousness, and uniformity that characterize the high school press. It has created

---

8. For a discussion of the studies, see Chapter V of this book.
9. Jack Nelson, ed., *Captive Voices: High School Journalism in America*, The Report of the Commission of Inquiry into High School Journalism (New York: Schocken Books, 1974), p. 47.
10. *Ibid.*, p. 48.

a high school press that in most cases is no more than a house organ for the school administration.[11]

The book aroused a storm of protest from administrators and advisers who charged it was a "witch hunt" by liberals who based their findings more on gut feelings than on solid research.[12] Indeed, the work does seem long on conclusions and short on substantiation. The sweeping findings were based mostly on a series of interviews around the country with disgruntled editors and on the results of three unscientific or poorly-designed surveys. The commission offered little evidence that its findings of overwhelming censorship at some schools, as reported in the hearings, were representative of public high schools in general.

One result of *Captive Voices* was that the Robert F. Kennedy Memorial opened the Student Press Law Center in Washington, D.C. The SPLC advises students facing censorship difficulties and publishes a quarterly newsletter of recent court cases relating to censorship in high school and college publications. The newsletter, like the other trade publications aimed at high school journalists, focuses on specific court findings with little examination of the larger philosophical issues.

This study borrows from this literature but seeks to do more than summarize it. The tone here is not impartial but concurs with the liberal approach described above. This approach will be developed further in subsequent chapters and will be a common theme throughout the book. I will argue that as students advance from primary schools to secondary schools, they should be entrusted with more and more rights, and that by the time they reach high school, student journalists should have the same First Amendment rights as professional reporters.

---

11. *Ibid.*
12. Louis Werner, "Captive Voices: Are They Still?" *Communication: Journalism Education Today*, Vol. 12, No. 3 (spring 1979), p. 4. See also John Bowen, "'Captive Voices' Brings new Study," *Communication: Journalism Education Today*, Vol. 9 (Spring 1976), pp. 18-22.

II

Surveys of Censorship

To understand the importance and persistence of censorship one must go to the schools and study the matter empirically. A half-dozen surveys conducted in the last 15 years have demonstrated that censorship is an institution in public high schools. This institution exists not just in the sense of principals excising articles and reprimanding editors, but also in the sense of the climate of intimidation and conformism that stifles creativity and critical analysis in high school newspapers. At the deepest level, censorship is rooted in small, provincial communities that place a premium on order and distrust nonconformism. Not only does censorship flourish in these communities, but often editors reflect the same values and are so deferential that they themselves avoid controversy and criticism of the school. Censorship and self-censorship are embedded in deeply-held community values and are not easily uprooted.

Unfortunately, most of the surveys conducted in secondary schools were poorly designed and are not statistically reliable. Most were confined to a single state or region, and many had very small samples or poor response rates. Comparison of results from different surveys is hindered because the surveys asked different questions and measured censorship in different ways. Therefore it is virtually impossible to compare results or to use one of the past surveys to estimate the general degree of censorship in the United States at a particular time. These surveys also were marred by a theoretical flaw, for they conceived of censorship too narrowly. They focused exclusively on incidents where the principal or adviser forbade publication of an article and ignored intimidation and

9

pressures that coerced the students themselves into altering or suppressing articles.

One of the earliest quantitative studies was conducted in 1965, before *Tinker* was decided, and is important because it assessed censorship and attitudes before advisers and principals were legally obliged to respect student rights. In this survey, questionnaires were mailed to the principals, advisers and student editors at the 224 public and parochial high schools in Los Angeles County, California. Responses were received from 91 principals, 92 advisers and 94 editors, a response rate of about 41 percent. All principals and all advisers said they had the authority to censor, although 55 percent of the principals and 36 percent of the advisers said they never used this authority. Among principals, 1 percent said they frequently censored articles, 7 percent said they seldom censored articles and 37 percent said they had censored articles once or twice. Three percent of the advisers said they frequently censored copy, 18 percent said they seldom censored, and 43 percent said they had censored once or twice.

Among all 277 respondents, only one--an adviser--said that to "support and reflect the proper image of the school" is not the role of a school newspaper. All the others, including students and principals, essentially felt the newspaper should be at least in part a public relations tool. However, one may not safely extrapolate from these results to conditions in the United States before *Tinker*, both because the survey was confined to one unrepresentative county and because results from parochial schools were mixed with results from public schools.[1]

Another early study was conducted in Arizona in 1969, the same year that *Tinker* was decided. Ninety-five high school newspaper advisers returned questionnaires (it is unclear how many originally were sent out), yielding the following results: 6.3 percent had no school newspaper; 11.5 percent reported no censorship and said editors were not criticized for running controversial articles; 25.3 percent reported no censorship but said there might be if the newspaper tried to be more controversial; and 56.9 percent reported either prior

---

1. Don D. Horine, "How Principals, Advisers and Editors View the High School Newspaper," *Journalism Quarterly*, Vol. XLIII (Summer 1966), pp. 339-45.

10

restraint or punishments after publication of controversial articles. The questions were ambiguous, however, so the last category could include not just prior restraint but also legitimate editing for style by the adviser, and a post-publication "punishment" could have been as slight as a principal expressing disappointment in a pupil.[2]

A 1973 survey of 700 newspaper advisers by the Commission of Inquiry into High School Journalism looked at the related question of who has final control of the content of the school newspaper. The commission sent the survey to 700 randomly-selected members of the Journalism Education Association and received 388 surveys back, a 55 percent response rate. It may be that the sample pool was unrepresentative of newspaper advisers in general, both because of the response rate and because members of the JEA tend to come from larger, more urban school districts where high school journalism is taken more seriously. Of the advisers who responded, 66.5 percent said they had the final right of approval of articles in the school paper, 16.6 percent said the student editor had final approval and 17.0 percent said the administration had final approval. In addition, 37.2 percent of the advisers said they limited the subject areas that could be covered in the paper and 29.7 percent said the administration limited what could be covered. The advisers were not asked how often they actually felt called upon to exercise their right of final approval or disapproval.[3]

Despite a 1972 decision by the U.S. Court of Appeal for the Seventh Circuit that prior restraints on high school newspapers are unconstitutional,[4] a 1976 survey found the ruling had little if any effect on schools in the circuit (Illinois, Indiana and Wisconsin). Only 15 percent of the principals and 10 percent of the advisers in the survey knew of the court

2. Max H. James, "Propaganda or Education? Censorship and School Journalism," *Arizona English Bulletin*, Vol. 13, No. 1 (October 1970), pp. 37-41. EDRS Document ED 045 675.
3. These statistics are based on data in Appendix B of Jack Nelson, ed., *Captive Voices: High School Journalism in America*, The Report of the Commission of Inquiry into High School Journalism (New York: Schocken books, 1974).
4. Fujishima v. Board of Education, 460 F.2d 1355.

decision, and the administrators still reviewed controversial articles at half the schools surveyed. Unfortunately, the sample of 474 respondents (principals and editors) represented a response rate of only 13 percent, not enough for reliable statistical inference.[5]

A 1978 survey of all 172 Illinois public high schools with more than 1,000 students (70 percent or 121 schools responded) also found that court cases had little impact on school policies towards student newspapers. At 3 percent of the schools the principal read all articles before they were published and at another 40 percent of the schools administrators read "controversial" articles before they appeared-- presumably so they could be censored. The journalism teacher who conducted the survey, James J. Nyka, concluded that "many newspaper advisers and administrators appear either unaware of students' constitutionally-protected rights, or have simply chosen to ignore them, hoping that the legal pendulum will swing the other way."[6]

Other surveys have substantiated the finding that teachers and administrators resist or are unaware of court decisions forbidding censorship. A 1977 poll of 400 members of the professional association of educators, Phi Delta Kappa, found that only 51 percent of the teachers were aware of students' rights of free expression (100 returned the surveys for a response rate of 25%). The respondents had an average of 14 years of professional experience and as association members probably were more aware than most of their peers.[7] Another survey, conducted of a nationwide sample in 1971, showed high school teachers favored

---

5. The survey was conducted by Robert Trager, Donna L. Dickerson and Dennis Jarvis, and was funded by the Student Press Law Center. "Survey Reveals Little Change in Censorship Following Ruling Banning Prior Restraint," *Student Press Law Center Report*, No. 4 (Spring 1977), p. 1.
6. "'Press' Four-Letter Word in Illinois," *Student Press Law Center Report*, Spring 1978, p. 9; James J. Nyka, "Censorship of Illinois High School Papers," *Communication: Journalism Education Today*, Vol. 12, No. 4 (summer 1979), pp. 6-9; and Lawrence B. Fuller, "Students' Rights of Expression: The Decade Since *Tinker*," *The English Journal*, Vol. 68, No. 9 (December 1979), pp. 11-14.

censorship by a margin of 70.7 percent to 16.9 percent, with 12.4 percent undecided.[8]

To determine if principals are aware of court rulings against censorship, two Louisiana State University researchers surveyed one nation-wide sample of principals in 1977 and another in 1979 to test their knowledge of First Amendment rights in secondary schools. The researchers posed nine hypothetical questions, involving controversial articles planned for the school newspaper, and asked the principals if they thought they legally could censor the articles. In eight of the nine cases censorship was not legally permissible. In 1977 the principals averaged 55 percent correct on each question; in 1979 the average was 44 percent correct, indicating that on the average a majority of the principals thought they could censor when legally they could not. However, the questions were worded differently in 1977 and 1979, in some cases very differently. Therefore it is unhelpful to compare the samples, and the statistics are valuable only individually, not as a time series. The figues do show that in both cases many principals (56 percent in response to the 1979 questions) either believe they may censor when they legally may not or are unsure of the law.[9]

---

7. Perry A. Zirkel, "A Test on Supreme Court Decisions Affecting Education," *Phi Delta Kappan,* Vol. 59, No. 8 (April 1978), pp. 521-22.
8. The number of respondents and the response rate are not mentioned. "Teacher Opinion Poll," *Today's Education,* Vol. 61, No. 3 (March 1972), p. 13.
9. A comparison of the results of the two surveys, and the questions asked in the second survey, are in E. Joseph Broussard and C. Robert Blackmon, "Principals Think They Can Do What Congress Cannot--Abridge Freedom of the High School Press," *Quill and Scroll,* October-November 1980, pp. 15-17. The results of the first survey, and the questions asked, are in E. Joseph Broussard and C. Robert Blackmon, "Advisers, Editors and Principals Judge First Amendment Cases," *Journalism Quarterly,* Vol. 55, No. 4 (winter 1978), pp. 797-99. In the 1977 survey principals at 126 high schools were polled and 42 responded for a response rate of 33 percent. In the 1979 survey, questionnaires were sent to a new sample of 260 principals, but the authors do not say how many responded. Although the authors compare the means for the two surveys, the

These are the principal surveys of censorship in secondary schools.[10] They are useful in examining the issue of censorship empirically if one is cautious in relying upon the data.[11] None of these surveys had a large, national sample and successfully measured how much censorship, in the broadest sense, existed in public high schools. The survey conducted for this study, therefore, is the first that may be reliably used to estimate the degree of censorship in public high schools in the United States.

Six-page questionnaires comprising 29 questions were mailed in October 1980 to 500 randomly-selected public

questions were worded differently, based on a comparison of the text of the 1977 questions in the *Journalism Quarterly* article and the 1979 questions in the *Quill and Scroll* article.

10. There also were at least two other surveys on the subject. One was conducted in 1977 but attempted to extrapolate from a sample of only 22 editors, 29 principals and 43 advisers (questionnaires had been sent to 175 of each, for response rates of 13 percent, 17 percent and 25 percent, respectively). Not only were the samples very small, but they were not selected randomly, so it would be extremely risky to make inferences based on this survey. John Bowen, *"Captive Voices* Brings New Study," *Communication: Journalism Education Today,* Vol. 9 (spring 1976), pp. 18-22. A 1977 survey by the National Council of Teachers of English (with a response rate of 30 percent resulting in a sample of 630) found some newspaper censorship at 32 percent of the respondents' schools. However, the questions were poorly designed and the respondents were English teachers rather than newspaper advisers. Lee Burress, "A Brief Report of the 1977 NCTE Censorship Survey," in James E. Davis, ed., *Dealing With Censorship* (Urbana, Ill.: NCTE, 1979), pp. 14-47.

11. The dangers of relying too much upon survey data are illustrated by a 1974 high school sex survey that shocked the school and community when 80 percent of the freshmen reported they had engaged in oral sex. Subsequent interviews determined that the students had thought that oral sex meant kissing. Donal Brown, "Everything You've Always Wanted to Know About Doing a Sex Survey," *Scholastic Editor,* Vol. 58, No. 2 (October/November 1978), p. 29.

high schools around the country.[12] Each state and the District of Columbia was represented with at least one school; Texas had the most with 41 schools. Nationally there are 25,378 schools with secondary grades,[13] so the randomly-selected pool of 500 represented almost 2 percent of the national total. Schools that did not respond to the first survey were sent a second questionnaire with a new cover letter in mid-December. Eventually 358 surveys were returned, an initial response rate of 71.6 percent. Then 27 of the schools that had not responded were telephoned to determine if their conditions were measurably different from those at schools that had returned the questionnaires. One-third of the schools telephoned had not returned the questionnaires because they had no school newspaper. Among those that did have newspapers, differences between the telephone sample and the regular sample were slight and not statistically significant. However, editors could not come to the telephone at six schools, so the telephone sample may not have been entirely representative. The total number of survey responses, including the telephone interviews, was 385 out of 500, a response rate of 77.7 percent. The sample is large enough and the response rate high enough so that the survey results may be considered reliable for statistical inference.

Fifty-eight of the mail responses (16 percent) and nine of the telephone responses (33 percent) reported that the school had no student newspaper. Additionally, 34 survey forms could not be included in the results because they were filled out by advisers rather than editors. In many cases the advisers explained that an editor had not yet been selected or was not available, and the responses of the advisers did not differ markedly from those of the students, but it was judged most prudent not to include the advisers' answers in the sample for quantitative analysis. Therefore, after

---

12. Judging from the names and addresses of the schools, they were sent to a true cross section of America. One survey was sent to Hot Springs High School in the town of Truth or Consequences, New Mexico. Another went to Thompson Falls High School (address: East of Thompson Falls, Thompson Falls, MT 59873). And quite randomly, a survey was sent to Peoria High School in Peoria, Illinois.

13. *Digest of Education Statistics 1979* (Washington, D.C.: National Council for Education Statistics, 1979), table 9, p. 13.

excluding schools that did not have newspapers and questionnaires filled out by advisers, 278 surveys remained to be analyzed in the sample.

The survey, while generally designed to assess the extent of censorship and determine predictors of censorship, was specifically aimed to test the hypothesis that censorship is most common in traditional communities--those areas, often in the country or small towns, where schools are small, students are usually deferential and high school journalism is not taken very seriously. It was hypothesized that traditional communities are most common in the South and West and are disproportionately composed of working class families.

The reason for offering this hypothesis is that traditional communities are insulated from liberal pressures and are unlikely to be aware of or responsive to liberal court rulings. Working class neighborhoods, as well as communities in the South and West, are likely to value order and discipline over student freedom. Moreover, small schools in what might be termed the "backwaters" of America are unlikely to undergo rigorous inspection of their policies by parents or the media, so no one may raise a fuss if the school does not obey the Supreme Court's interpretations of the First Amendment. Finally, in such small schools and traditional communities, the students themselves are likely to defer to school authorities and may not write anything worth censoring, or if they do, they may submit to the censorship without argument.

Censorship was measured on an index based on the results of six questions. Those questions are listed below with the number of points assigned to each response for calculating the index (more points mean more censorship). The proportions of student editors who chose each response do not always add up to 100 percent because of rounding and because occasionally a respondent skipped a few questions on the questionnaire.[14]

1. Has there been any censorship of a student publication at your school in the last three years? (Please circle your answer.)

---

14. The complete questionnaire, with results for each question, appears in the Appendix.

47.5% (0 points) a) no censorship

33.1% (1 point)   b) one or two incidents of censorship in three years

12.6% (2 points) c) three to ten incidents of censorship in three years

5.8%   (3 points) d) there has been repeated and continual censorship

3. Does the newspaper adviser or school administration discourage the newspaper from probing in controversial areas?

32.4% (1 point)   a) yes

66.5% (0 points) b) no

4. How restricted is your newspaper in covering sensitive subjects?

18.0% (0 points) a) Completely unrestricted. I can't imagine any censorship here.

76.3% (1 point)   b) Somewhat restricted. The school might not let us cover some subjects but for the most part we are allowed to write what we want.

4.7%   (2 points) c) Very restricted. The administration lets us print only what it likes to see.

5. Suppose the newspaper staff wanted to print the following in an editorial: "Far too much money at this school goes for athletics and not nearly enough to academics. The school administration has the wrong priorities, and until things get straightened out a diploma from here will not mean much." Do you think you would be permitted to write that in your school paper?

56.1% (0 points) a) yes

18.7% (2 points) b) no

24.5% (1 point)   c) not sure

[Question 9 said, "Suppose you heard that a half-dozen parents were circulating a petition demanding that the principal be fired. Would you..."]

10. Regardless of your answer above, suppose you decided to include a major article on the front page about the petition drive and criticisms of the principal. Do you think the administration would let you do this?

36.3% (0 points)   a) yes

32.4% (2 points)   b) no

30.6% (1 point)   c) not sure

11. Would you be worried that if you tried to run such an article about the principal it might be censored or the administration might try to punish you or the newspaper?

58.6% (1 point)   a) yes

39.6% (0 points)   b) no

    The censorship index had a possible range from 0 to 11 points. About 5.8 percent of the schools had the minimum, indicating no censorship and almost no potential for censorship, and 1.7 percent had the maximum, indicating very heavy censorship. The mean score on the index was 4.2 with a standard deviation of 2.7. The censorship index was a far more reliable indicator of the state of freedom of the press at a school than was the number of incidents of censorship in the last three years. Many editors who reported no incidents of censorship said in response to the other questions they would be censored if they wrote something controversial. For example, 22.8 percent of those who reported no incidents of censorship said they were discouraged from probing in controversial areas. Two-thirds of those who reported no incidents of censorship said they were somewhat restricted in covering sensitive subjects. In response to the hypothetical situation in question 10, fewer than half said they thought they would be permitted to print a major article on the front page about a petition drive against the principal. Clearly the reason many editors reported no incidents of censorship was that the students never wrote anything sufficiently controversial to warrant censorship. This points to a shortcoming of many previous surveys that attempted to assess censorship by asking advisers how frequently they censored copy.

The independent variables used to measure the association between the censorship index and traditional communities were based on questions about school size, the character of the community, the editors' attitudes about student rights, and the production schedule and relative professionalism of the newspaper. One difficulty in attempting to assess the value of any individual factor as a predictor of censorship is multicollinearity--many of the independent variables are strongly correlated. For example, schools with large student bodies tend to be three-year schools in large cities, while very small schools tend to have many grades and usually are located in the country or in small towns. Therefore it is difficult to isolate the impact of any single independent variable because of the overlap among them.

The survey results show that school size is inversely related to censorship, as was predicted by the hypothesis. The correlation between student body population and the censorship index is -.22, and the simple regression equation is $y = 5.0 - .0008x$, where y is the score on the censorship index and x is the student body population.[15] The regression is statistically significant at the .0005 level and explains 4.3 percent of the variance.[16] The x coefficient may seem small, but its impact may be quite significant because of the range in size of x (student bodies ranged from 30 to 6,000). For example, a large school with 2,000 more students than a smaller one would be expected to have a score on the censorship index of 1.6 points lower than that of the smaller school. Transforming the student body populations into logarithmic values only very slightly increased the correlation and regression coefficients, and plots showed no significant curvilinear relation between school size and censorship score that would not have been picked up by linear analysis.

---

15. The student body is measured as the reported number of students in the school if it is a three- or four-year high school, or as the number of students in the top four grades if the school includes more than four grades.

16. The figures for the percent of variance explained are adjusted for degrees of freedom. The figures would be slightly higher if they were just the dividend of the explained sum of squares divided by the total sum of squares.

Another measure of school size, the number of grades in the school, revealed a smaller but also statistically significant relationship with the censorship index. When school size was measured with one point for three-year schools, two points for four-year school and three points for schools with five or more grades, the correlation with the censorship index was .16. The regression equation, $y = 3.0 + .69x$, was statistically significant at the .01 level and explained 2.0 percent of the variance. Therefore, both measures of school size show small schools--whether measured in terms of few students or many grades--have more censorship than large schools.

The relationship between censorship and size of the community is less important. The correlation between the censorship index and size of the community is .10, when one point is assigned to a city with a population of more than 150,000, two points to a smaller city or suburbs and three points to the country. The simple regression equation, $y = 3.3 + .47x$, explains 0.5 percent of the variance and is significant only at the .1 level.

A much stronger association is evident between the degree of censorship and the class character of the community (as reported by the student editor). When one point is assigned for upper middle class, two points for middle class and three points for working class, the correlation between that score and the censorship index is .19. The regression equation is $y = 2.5 + .83x$, which is statistically significant at the .001 level and explains 3.3 percent of the variance. Analysis of the differences in means also shows markedly greater censorship in working class communities than in middle class and upper middle class communities.

When the three most promising elements discussed above--student body population, number of grades in the school and class character of the community--are combined in a multiple regression equation, the result is $y = 2.8 - .0006x_1 + .36x_2 + .67x_3$, where y is the censorship index score, x_1 is the student body pop-population, x_2 is the number of grades in the school on a three-point scale (same scales as before). The coefficient for number of grades is no longer statistically significant, but the other two coefficients are significant at the .01 level. This regression explains 6.7 percent of the variance, which is better than any of the simple regressions but still leaves much unexplained.

The professionalism of a school newspaper also is a useful predictor of censorship. Certainly "professionalism" is somewhat subjective and is difficult to quantify, but some factors are associated with more professional school publications: commercial printing, frequent editions and a willingness to cover controversies and criticize school officials. The correlation between censorship and method of printing (1 point for commercial printing, two points for duplication within the school) is .13. The regression equation is y = 3.3 + .76x, which explains 1.2 percent of the variance and is statistically significant at the .025 level. The correlation between the censorship index and frequency of publication is very slight and is not statistically significant, perhaps because newspapers that come out very infrequently (such as a few times per year) are so unprofessional and non-controversial that school officials feel no need to censor them.

A far stronger, inverse, relationship is evident between willingness to cover controversies and the degree of censorship. To some extent this is obvious. Only a newspaper that is not heavily censored can cover controversies. However, the questions that assessed willingness to cover controversies were able partially to isolate the innate aggressiveness or deference of the editor from his reaction to the constraints imposed upon him. Those questions were as follows:

9. Suppose you heard that a half-dozen parents were circulating a petition demanding that the principal be fired. Would you:

    35.3%   a)   wait and see what happens
    29.5%   b)   assign a reporter and ask him or her to write a small article
    34.2%   c)   assign one or more reporters and ask them to write a major article

12. Suppose a group of students known as the "smokers" (because they smoked cigarettes near the school during the lunch hour) threatened to boycott classes because of harassment by school staff. What would you do?

    22.3%   a)   probably nothing for now
    43.9%   b)   write a short article
    32.0%   c)   write a long article

13. How would you describe your newspaper?

    28.4%   a)   Not controversial. Covers positive school news and does not criticize teachers or school officials.

    68.0%   b)   Sometimes controversial. Includes some news or editorials critical of school staff.

    2.5%   c)   Often controversial. Includes news or editorials strongly critical of school staff and makes little effort to be "polite."

14. If you responded a or b above, why is the newspaper not more controversial? (Circle as many as apply.)

    23.6%   a)   I don't think a school newspaper should spend much time criticizing the school or people who work in it.

    13.3%   b)   We're not allowed to be more controversial.

    50.9%   c)   Other [The two most common responses were, first, that there are few controversies to cover at the school and second, that school newspapers should focus on positive news. A few editors said that if they were more controversial their advisers would be fired.]

    3.3%   a and b

    3.3%   a and c

    1.5%   b and c

    0.7%   a, b and c

The two hypothetical questions asked for the editors' initial response to a news event without considering the possibility of censorship. Moreover, only 18.9 percent of the editors said a reason their newspapers are not more controversial is censorship. Thus, while censorship has some chilling effect that results in editors not bothering to cover controversies, it also is clear that many students decide of their own volition to avoid controversial news. The hypothesis tested here predicts an inverse relationship between inclination to cover controversies and degree of censorship, because in traditional communities students are deferential and unlikely to dredge up "bad" news.

The data confirm this inverse relationship, for the correlations between the censorship index and the hypothetical questions about the principal and "smokers" are -.27 and -.16, respectively. The simple regression equation for the question about the principal (where answers a, b and c are coded 1, 2 and 3, respectively) is $y = 6.0 - .86x$, which is statistically significant at the .0001 level and explains 6.8 percent of the variance. The regression equation for the other question, about "smokers," is $y = 5.4 - .57x$, where x is coded 1, 2 and 3 for a, b and c, respectively. The coefficient is statistically significant at the .01 level and the equation explains 2.0 percent of the variance. The combined regression equation is $y = 6.6 - .79x_1 - .38x_2$, where x_1 is the hypothetical question about the principal and x_2 is the question about "smokers." The equation explains 7.5 percent of the variance, but only the coefficient for the "principal" question is statistically significant at the .05 level.

The level of controversy in the newspaper is an even better predictor of censorship. This is partly because only uncensored newspapers could be controversial, but also because this reflects the innate aggressiveness of the editors, of the same sort as that measured by the hypothetical questions discussed above. More than three-quarters of the editors who described their newspapers as "not controversial" said their newspapers would not be appreciably more controversial even if they were not censored. Therefore the level of controversy in a school newspaper seems to reflect student attitudes more than censorship.

The editors' evaluations of the level of controversy in their newspapers (when a, b and c are coded 1, 2 and 3, respectively) has a correlation of -.34 with the censorship index. The simple regression is $y = 7.4 - 1.8x$, which is statistically significant at the .0001 level and explains 10.8 percent of the variance. The multiple regression of the two hypothetical questions and the level of controversy is $y = 8.6 - .54x_1 - .34x_2 - 1.5x_3$, where x_1 refers to the hypothetical about the principal, x_2 to the hypothetical about the "smokers" and x_3 to the degree of controversy in the newspaper. The coefficients are statistically significant at the .05 level and the regression explains 14.1 percent of the variance. This confirms the hypothesis that deferential editors, who steer away from controversy and who are found most frequently in traditional communities, are most likely to suffer censorship.

The same association between deference and censorship also shows up strongly in the responses to two other questions. Those questions are:

15. What rights do you think you should have?

    54.0%   a) same rights as adult newspaper reporters and editors

    42.8%   b) some rights, but under supervision of the school administration

    1.8%   c) the administration should have final authority over the newspaper

18. Suppose an article you write this year is censored. What would you do?

    28.4%   a) nothing

    58.6%   b) complain and perhaps circulate petitions

    7.9%   c) take the case to court

The correlation between question 15 and the censorship index is .2, when a, b and c are coded 1, 2 and 3, respectively. The regression equation is $y = 2.7 + x$, which is statistically significant at the .001 level and explains 3.7 percent of the variance. This means that editors who are constrained think they should have fewer rights, while editors who have greater freedom believe they should have those freedoms. It also means that students who are censored today probably will be the censors of tomorrow.

The correlation between question 18 and the censorship index is even stronger, -.35 (where a, b and c are coded 1, 2 and 3, respectively). The regression equation is $y = 7.2 - 1.7x$, which is significant at the .0001 level and explains 11.6 percent of the variance. One reason the second correlation is so high is probably psychological: An editor who has never been censored is more likely to be outraged at the idea than one who has grown accustomed to censorship. But there is more to it than that--the deferential editors who would do nothing upon being censored are most likely to come from small, traditional communities where obedience and respect for authority are inculcated into most youngsters. This is indicated by a very strong correlation of .41 between student body population and an editor's reaction if censored.

The only aspect of the hypothesis not confirmed by the data is the prediction that the West and South have the most censorship. Instead, the West had the least censorship, followed by the Central States, the East and the South. The means for the censorship index, by region, are as follows:

West	3.1
Central States	4.5
East	4.5
South	4.7

This is surprising, for the West would have seemed likely to include traditional, conservative communities with small schools and deferential students--the ingredients of censorship, according to the results of the other questions. However, it should be noted that the differences in means are minimal, and only the West is different from any of the others by a statistically significant margin. Because the others are essentially not different from each other, the East, South and Central States may be seen as approximately the same in terms of censorship, with the West having markedly less censorship.

This may perhaps be explained by the tradition of individualism and respect for non-conformism in the West. Furthermore, the East probably should not have been expected to have significantly less censorship than the other regions. The liberalism, mobility and urban character associated with the East--all factors that work against censorship--are true only of the cities in the East. The schools that were surveyed in the East included some schools in large cities but also included many in tiny farm towns along the Eastern seaboard. Also, the conservative, agrarian character of the East probably was exaggerated in this survey because of the nature of the random selection. A large city will have a few very large high schools, while in the country there are many very small high schools--yet each school has the same chance of being selected. Therefore, rural communities will receive more weight in a random survey of high schools than they would in a random survey of people.

The survey revealed some further information. Student newspapers experience far more censorship than other student publications, although this may have been magnified because the respondents were student newspaper editors who would have been most aware of newspaper censorship. More than 81 percent of those who reported censorship said the censorship was exclusively in the student newspaper, and another 10 percent said there was censorship in the student newspaper and in other publications. Only 2.7 percent reported censorship of an underground newspaper in the last three years.

The editors clearly were aware of at least some of their First Amendment rights. More than 90 percent said they had a legal right to print the hypothetical editorial criticism of the school's devotion to athletics. Most of the remaining 10 percent were unsure, and only 1.1 percent said they did not have a legal right to print the criticism. However, many editors commented in the margin that they would have a right to print the statement only if it could be proven--apparently not realizing that the statement was an opinion and could not possibly be proven one way or the other. This was a frequent theme, for editors often commented that they should be permitted to write what is true, without recognizing that truth in almost all editorials and some articles is subjective and outside the realm of what is provable.

More than four-fifths of the editors said they were somewhat familiar or very familiar with their legal rights of expression. About 64 percent said administrators at their schools believed they had legal rights of freedom of the press. However, only a small minority of editors said they had the final right of approval of articles and advertisements in their newspapers--an important test of the real level of freedom in the school. Only 14 percent said the students had final approval, 18.3 percent said the administration had final approval and 62.2 percent said the adviser had final control. This indicates a strong potential for censorship at the 81 percent of schools where the adviser or administration has final authority over the newspaper. This also supports the suspicion that many schools have had no troubles with censorship only because students have not written anything critical or controversial.

Although most trade publications aimed at high school journalists urge schools to establish a written policy governing what may be printed in student publications, only 14.4 percent of the schools in the survey had such a written policy. The survey asked students to enclose a copy of their publications policy if they had one, and most did so. Most of the policies seemed to have been prepared by attorneys and adhered strictly to the standards set forth in *Tinker* and other cases. Therefore, a written publications policy does seem a good way to ensure that a school will abide by court rulings about free expression for high school students.

The survey also revealed some interesting descriptive statistics about high school newspapers. Slightly more than half in the survey are published monthly, 17 percent are published every two weeks and 7 percent appear weekly. The remaining 22 percent are published either every three weeks or as the spirit moves the staff (in some cases only twice a year). Almost 70 percent of the newspapers are printed commercially, and even among those duplicated within the school, many are reproduced on high-quality equipment. About half of the newspapers receive funding from the school; the rest fend for themselves by selling advertisements. Newspapers that did not receive funding were more likely than others to be censored, probably because most unfunded newspapers are in small schools (and traditional communities). Almost all newspapers in large, urban schools receive some funding.

In all types of schools, advisers may hold a few trump cards in controlling the content of the student newspaper: selection of the editor, assignment of stories or editing of stories. At 56.8 percent of the schools in the survey, the adviser alone selects the editor, and the adviser participates in the selection at another 14 percent of the schools. This is a source of enormous control over the newspaper, for by selecting a mild, deferential editor the adviser and principal will not have to bother with censorship. Yet there may be no preferable alternative, for the adviser probably knows better than anyone else the talents of the applicants for each position. Moreover, none of the respondents reported any abuse in the selection of editors (somewhat understandably, as the respondents were the editors), and the editors interviewed on the telephone were for the most part indignant at the suggestion that their adviser might choose an editor on any basis other than merit.

In general, most editors seemed content with the roles taken by their advisers. Only 10.8 percent said their adviser would take the side of the administration in a conflict between the newspaper staff and the administration. On the other hand, 45 percent said the adviser would take the students' side, and the remainder said they were not sure or said the adviser would not take sides. In their comments, too, many students said their advisers had supported them in censorship conflicts with the administration, even at the risk of losing their jobs or, as one student put it, "get[ting] transferred on permanent bus duty."

The students were invited to comment at the end of the survey, and the majority did, often at considerable length. Their comments were fascinating, both because they provided a glimpse of conditions behind the statistics and because they illuminated the deference of student editors in many small schools and traditional communities. The students first told of the kinds of articles that had been censored--most often teenage sex features, student opinion polls, articles about faculty or staff labor unions, uncomplimentary references to students or staff, investigative articles and editorial criticisms of school officials or policies. Two comments are typical:

> We seem to have the most trouble with censorship at our school when we try to print something sexually oriented. Recently we wanted to print a medically-based article on "hickeys" (the dangers of them) and our principle [sic] would not allow it to be printed in a "newspaper that I supervise!" We have ran [sic] into similar problems with rape, contraceptives, and teenage pregnancy. Last year we had 13 pregnancies in our school and we feel something should be done.
> Another area of censorship is criticizing the athletic department in any way. Our school is very sports oriented and a lot of "funny" things go on with money and players and a few of the coaches. Our adviser, of course, won't let us dig and come up with anything good for fear the principle [sic] would stop our publication.

* * *

> Our newspaper has been the victim of instance after instance of censorship. Last year, several members of our staff were called to the principal's office to hear [sic] several of the feature articles which he censored totally from the paper, because he felt they were in poor taste. We took a newspaper survey on the biggest problems in our school, and many of the responses included smoking in the lavs. Our principal would not allow us to print these results, because he said they gave a

bad impression of the school.

We would like to fight our administration on the issue of censorship but are afraid the situation would become worse. Our adviser cannot risk fighting the administration, because [sic] has not received her tenure. As students, a major disagreement with the administration could cost us our reputations with our teachers.

Many students mentioned this desire to avoid incurring the principal's displeasure, and administrators clearly exploited the students' meekness. Instead of blatantly forbidding the staff to print certain specific articles, many principals use their positions of authority to intimidate editors into acquiescence. Occasionally the threats are explicit; more often they are implicit: that the adviser might be fired, that the newspaper might be shut down, or simply that the editors might fall into disfavor. Even the last threat can be frightening to an adolescent trying to impress the chief authority figure in his school, so this intimidation has a "chilling effect" that keeps the students in line. This is one reason why censorship cannot be measured simply by the number of stories that the adviser or principal has forbidden students to print. Intimidation is censorship, too, as described in these examples:

There were very few times the principal actually said, "you cannot print this story." What he would do is keep me in his office hassling me and wearing me down 'til I would finally say, "I give up, I will not print the story." He would literally keep me in his office for hours.

* * *

Each deadline, before bringing the copy to the typesetter, we must take it all before the principal. He always has negative comments to make, although so far this year we have not been prevented from printing anything. It's his way of embarrassing us into printing harmless material. I can remember thinking, "What will Mr. ___ think of this? I wonder if I should tone it down a bit."

* * *

There has really been no "censorship" of our newspaper, *per se,* but the administration does pressure us not to print matters that would "rock

29

157159

the boat," so to speak. We are allowed a fair amount of freedom in what we write, yet it sometimes feels that there's an omnipresent hand over our head, not actually telling us what we can print and what we cannot, but letting us know all the same.

* * *

Censorship here is more implied than express. Pressure is brought to bear upon the adviser, an untenured second-year teacher, rather than the students. For example, when the administration learned the paper was planning an article on the controversial demotion of a choir director, the adviser was called into his principal's office and was told the school superintendent felt such an article would not be appropriate for a school paper.

Students--and advisers--submit to this kind of intimidation because they do not want to make waves and offend conservative teachers and administrators with whom they may be friendly. This is especially true in a small school and traditional community, where there is a strong pressure to conform to conventional standards and mores. Because everyone knows everyone else in small towns, a dispute in the school over censorship easily may have reverberations throughout the community. An editor may simply feel it is not worth it to risk his reputation and start a feud for the sake of an article that anyway would cause an uproar if it were printed. One editor from a small, Midwestern town wrote:

Since our school is small and everyone knows everyone else, it is quite difficult to criticize a teacher or student and see them day after day in class. I'm afraid there would not only be hard feelings between the newspaper staff and the offended party but also between families and church groups involved.

It is this sort of caution and desire to avoid a fuss that makes editors in small, rural schools prime targets for censorship. In many cases, such editors are so deferential that they write nothing worth censoring. This may be true for two reasons: First, a student editor may wish to avoid being ostracized as a maverick or non-conformist who criticizes the school and unearths controversies. This might be termed a deference of convenience. Second, an editor reared in a traditional community may have developed a genuine deference based on the same conservative values as those held by his parents, teachers and principal. In this case, the student believes that the school newspaper should be positive and should support the school, so he does not need to be intimidated or pressured. The editor will--like many small-town commercial newspaper editors--avoid controversies because they might besmirch the name of the school or community. Whether the deference is genuine or one of convenience, the result is a self-censorship as stifling as any restrictions imposed by a school administration. Following are some students' comments revealing the insipid influence of deference:

At _____, the staff, the adviser and the administration get along really well. The administration is willing to answer any questions in an interview, and they are always supportive of our paper. They are sent a copy of our newspaper a day before the student body receives theirs and they critique it and give us their comments. So, as for censorship, we (the staff and adviser) read each story so many times, that we make sure nothing like the threat of censorship ever happens. Common sense and the staff policy usually guarantees [sic] that nothing will be written that needs to be censored.

[genuine deference]

* * *

Our newspaper contains only class news, activities, entertainment, and things only dealing with our school. We are not so controversial because that only causes problems in the long run....The better you get along with the people you work with and the people you write about, the better off the newspaper will be. Getting along is what it's all about.

[deference of convenience]

* * *

As our paper represents our school, we try to give the best impression while representing all the facts. Some articles, if our adviser feels are very controversial, are taken to the administration for approval for publication. One example: A student had written to the editor complaining fiercely about her class not having a prom. The letter was

31

taken to the Superintendent. He suggested it not be printed, and if the student had complaints to come talk to him. We do not use our paper for students to air personal gripes and grudges against other students or instructors.

[genuine deference]

* * *

I would just like to note that, while I realize the obvious value of freedom of the press, it is my opinion that a high school newspaper must be placed in a category by itself; its function is to provide positive publicity for the school. While some controversial subjects are sometimes covered, the overall tone of the publication should remain supportive of the school.

[genuine deference]

The comments of these editors, and of many others like them, reveal just how pervasive censorship and self-censorship are in secondary schools across America. Even if all administrative censorship could be eliminated overnight, newspapers at many schools would be changed not at all. Almost 45 percent of editors said they should be supervised or controlled by the administration, and probably many of those who opposed censorship would not dream of ever writing anything worth censoring. Therefore it is naive to assume--as *Captive Voices* did--that the fundamental reason school newspapers are trivial and innocuous is that they are censored by school officials. In many schools, particularly small ones in traditional communities, triviality and innocuousness are rooted in the traditions of the school paper, and the students themselves reject the notion of change. They may not want to feel constrained, but even if all constraints were removed they would act little differently. After all, fewer than one-fifth of editors said censorship was the reason they were not more controversial. The rest said either that the school newspaper should be generally positive or that there was no controversy in the school (a view that reflects the same deferential outlook because if the editors were aggressive and dug for news they probably would find it).

Three factors may therefore be isolated to explain the vapid flavor of many high school newspapers. First, many schools experience censorship in its most blatant form, where the adviser or principal prohibits publication of specific articles or editorials. Second, the principal or adviser may, without actually forbidding publication of specific articles, cultivate a climate of intimidation in which the cruder form of censorship is unnecessary. Third, many editors in traditional communities possess a stultifying deference that keeps them away from anything that might offend or shock a reader.

This survey has shown censorship to be related to school size, town size, class character of the community, student deference and the degree of controversy in the school newspaper. Therefore, one might propose the following model to explain censorship:

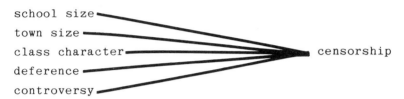

A five-way multiple regression based on all the above factors does indeed explain 16.6 percent of the variance, but in such a large regression only deference[17] and degree of controversy remain statistically significant. The other three factors—school size, town size and class character—all drop out because of overlap and are no longer statistically significant at the .05 level. However, these three factors still do seem important, both because individually they correlate with censorship and because they correlate with deference and degree of controversy, here shown to be the two factors most immediately associated with censorship. Therefore, one may hypothesize that deference and controversy are *directly* related to censorship, while school size, town size and class character are *indirectly* related to censorship. That model looks like this:

_____

17. Deference here is measured as the response to question 18 (the editor's reaction to censorship).

33

Every link in this model is secure, for strong relationships exist from one level to the next. School size, for example, has a correlation of .41 with deference and .32 with degree of controversy. The same model as above, with correlations included, is as follows:

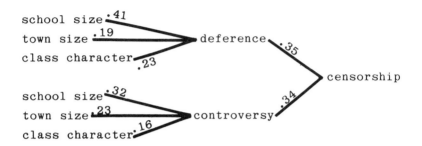

Of course, school size, town size and class character are simply the measures of traditional communities, so the above model may be reformulated as the impact of traditional communities on censorship, working through the intermediaries of deference and controversy. The reformulated model is as follows:

This model explains the positive relationships between traditional communities and censorship, but of course the relationship is not exact. Other unrelated factors may be important and may sometimes work at cross purposes with those reported here. Two factors that probably are very important are the attitudes toward censorship of the newspaper adviser and the school principal. While a traditional community may offer a hospitable climate for censorship, it is left to the principal and adviser actually to censor. Future studies therefore should examine attitudes of principals and advisers as probable predictors of censorship. It also would be worthwhile to go further and study ages and educational background of the principals and advisers as possible predictors of their attitudes.

Future researchers must change the ways in which they think about and measure censorship. It is insufficient to ask an adviser how frequently he or she censors articles. By that standard, almost half the schools in this survey would have had no censorship in the last three years. A better analysis would include three additional types of questions. First, hypothetical questions should be asked to find out if a lack of incidents of censorship merely indicates that students have written nothing controversial. Second, students should be asked if school officials intimidate or pressure them into avoiding controversy. Third, they should be asked who has the final say about content in the newspaper. Together these questions will provide an approximate reflection of the true state of freedom of the press in a high school, because each type of question focuses upon a different form of censorship or potential censorship.

So how should censorship, in the broadest sense, be assessed in the United States based on this survey? Fewer than 19 percent of the editors said they were completely unrestricted, and only 13.8 percent said students had the final right of approval of their newspaper's content. Only 6.9 percent of the schools scored at the minimum of the censorship index, indicating no censorship and virtually no potential for censorship. Therefore, while noting that about half of all public high schools have little overt censorship, this survey suggests that newspapers at more than 80 percent of all public high schools have some censorship and are somewhat constrained, although the exact proportion will depend upon the standard one sets.

It is striking how little change has occurred in censorship patterns during the last 15 years, as reported in different surveys. Exact figures cannot be compared, because different questions were asked and past surveys were either local or non-random, but the statistics of censorship do not seem to have diminished appreciably. One question that was worded almost the same in two surveys may be compared and shows almost no difference. Members of the Journalism Education Association were asked in the 1973 survey cited earlier who had the final right of approval of articles in the newspaper. The advisers responded: the adviser, 66.5 percent; the student editor, 16.5 percent; and the administration, 17.0 percent. In the survey for this book seven years later, the same question was asked, and the students responded: the adviser, 63.2 percent; the students, 13.8 percent; and the administration, 17.8 percent. The differences reveal no meaningful change over the last seven years in responses to this question. However, it must be emphasized that the answers to just one question in surveys may not be used to extrapolate that the state of freedom of the press in high schools did not change from 1973 to 1981.

The reason for the persistence of censorship is that it rests less on laws and court decisions than on attitudes and political cultures. Traditional schools are slow to obey unpopular Supreme Court decisions, especially where the issue has low visibility. Even if principals no longer scrutinize each article intended for publication, they often can control the newspaper by pressuring the staff and fostering a climate of intimidation that chills the creativity, aggressiveness and professionalism of student journalists. Even without such pressure or intimidation, many students voluntarily defer to the judgment of their adviser or principal because of their deeply felt aversion to conflict and controversy. Censorship and self-censorship, in other words, are institutionalized in most American public high schools.

High school journalism is in poor health--it is pallid, apathetic and bland--but new rules alone will not invigorate high school newspapers. Liberal court ruling such as *Tinker* were a necessary but not sufficient step to nurse the high school press to health. Attitudes--of students, principals and entire communities--will have to change before censorship, self-censorship and stultifying deference are rooted out. Only then will high school newspapers be fully free to realize their potential as a valuable adjunct of the fourth estate in the schools.

III

A Critique of Censorship

High school students stand at the threshold of
adulthood and therefore occupy an ambiguous niche in
society. No longer children, not yet adults, they
aspire to the rights and respect that are the
perquisites of adulthood, and they chafe at the
paternalism they feel they have outgrown. Society is
uncertain and contradictory in dealing with them, and
the result is confusion about their status and rights.
The juvenile justice system, for example, provides
youths with the right to an attorney and the right not
to testify against themselves, but within a
paternalistic setting in which a judge acts also as
jury. Drinking ages oscillate and demarcations of
adulthood vary substantially--teenagers pay "adult"
prices at the movie theater five years before they can
see "adult" movies. The confusion is compounded in the
schools, where some educators say rights should not
apply. The debate over rights for high school
journalists illuminates this gray area and illustrates
the confusion. This chapter will examine censorship
from a normative rather than a legal perspective:
Should there be censorship, and why or why not?[1]

The two critical issues in deciding whether high
school students should have freedom of expression are,
first, whether the students should be considered
primarily as children or primarily as adults, and
second, whether individual rights, even if they should
apply to people of high school age, necessarily should

---

1. This chapter will consider only the social
    arguments for and against censorship. The legal
    issues will be discussed in the next chapter.

extend into the schools. Liberal and conservative arguments derive from differing assumptions on these two questions. The liberals assume that high school students are closer to adulthood than childhood, and that schools must not be "enclave of totalitarianism."[2] The conservatives assume that high school students are children more than adults and that many rights should not apply to the schools because of the need to impart an education in an atmosphere of calm and order. How much freedom of expression high school students should have may be decided after examining the premises and arguments of each side.

The conservative view reflects an authoritarian tradition in education that sought to imbue youngsters with respect for their elders as a moral value. "Break the will," John Wesley wrote in the 18th century, "whatever pain it costs, break the will, if you would not damn the child."[3] This Puritan ethic equated respect with submission, so that it was considered disrespectful to disagree openly with an elder. This perspective clearly sees the student as a child who must be molded by the teacher into a sensible, deferential and moral person.

This approach, with its moral overtones, survives to some degree in many small schools and traditional communities--hence the deference found in the survey and reported in Chapter II. A modern statement of this justification for strict rules governing student conduct is provided by Lord James of Rusholme:

It must be remembered that the child demands security above anything else. And security includes a definite and comprehensive moral code. As any adult who finds himself in a position of authority knows, nothing is more exhausting than to be faced every day with a succession of choices, often moral ones. To lay this burden on the young is an abrogation of responsibility that can become deeply harmful. Thus an excessive libertarianism can bewilder and over-burden the child and replace the authority of the teacher by that of the herd, which

---

2.   Tinker v. Des Moines School District, 393 U.S. 503, 511.

3.   Quoted in Lord James of Rusholme, "Education," in Clifford Rhodes, ed., *Authority in a Changing Society* (London: Constable, 1969), pp. 62-63.

may be more capricious and more conformist, and is certainly less knowledgeable and experienced.[4]

Not only must children be restricted for their own good, but also for the good of others, the conservatives say. Students lack the wisdom and experience to exercise their freedoms properly and would abuse their liberties. The power of the press may be considerable, especially for ill, yet those who would publish the newspaper have little journalism experience and little stake in the school, especially if they are seniors. They may regret an indiscretion as soon as it is printed, but by then it is too late. Why risk the school's harmony and reputation on the whims of an inexperienced editor who may regret his follies as soon as he commits them? The school would not permit a science student to play at being a doctor, so why permit a journalism student to play at being a crusading reporter.[5] Certainly a bad student reporter can do almost as much harm--in terms of libel, invasions of privacy, distortions and sensationalism--as can an incompetent doctor.

The conservatives focus not only on the age and inexperience of high school students, but also on what they see as the special setting of the school. The mandate of the school, they say, is not to rear debators or sophists but to educate students. This role of educating students, as they see it, may best be fulfilled by maintaining order in the schools and authority in the teacher. A critical school newspaper might attack the principal or teachers, subverting their authority and sowing discontent among students. A strong-minded newspaper also will distract students from their academic studies--which is the principal reason they attend school. In this way an unrestrained school newspaper hurts not only staff but also students whose classes are disrupted by controversies engendered by the newspaper. Because students are in school for the specific purpose of learning from their teachers, the school should not be seen as a microcosm of society where students have the same individual rights as adults. Rather, public schools are a special case where

---

4. *Ibid.*, 64.
5. "If we do not allow free thinking in chemistry or biology, why should we allow it in morals or politics?" asked August Comte. Isaiah Berlin, *Four Essays on Liberty*, (Oxford: Oxford Univ. Press, 1969), p. 151.

constraints on expression are necessary to allow schools to fulfill their special purpose of educating the young. Order--and censorship--are necessary in the schools because a calm and respectful climate is most conducive to learning.

The conservative argument adds that because schools are special institutions designed to promote learning and not bickering, even the issue of freedom of expression is illusory. The school newspaper here is seen as a teaching tool, an opportunity for hands-on experience so that students may learn journalism skills. As in any other class, the authority is the teacher and ultimately the principal and school board. The school is supposed to teach the students good journalism, not allow them to indulge in whatever journalism they choose.

The final argument conservatives use to underscore the special status of schools is that censorship is necessary to screen for libel and obscenity and material that would offend the community. If school officials are criminally or civilly liable for articles published in the school newspaper, clearly they should be in a position to prevent this type of injury from occuring. It would be absurd to suggest that principals should be accountable in the courts for libelous articles that they could not censor if they wanted to.

Beyond what is legally culpable, the conservatives say, school administrators and school boards are responsible to the people in the school district, who in most cases pay school taxes and elect school boards. The voters, acting through their elected representatives, should be permitted some say in the school newspaper. Certainly citizens should not be forced to pay for a newspaper they vehemently oppose, subsidizing the vitriolic attacks of whoever happens to be editor, with no checks on his power.

This outlook would appeal to liberal sympathies in some circumstances. One can imagine the outrage in a liberal, racially-mixed community if a school newspaper editor used the paper as a platform from which to launch vicious racist attacks. The same uproar would occur in a liberal, heavily-Jewish community if a student newspaper editor wrote neo-Nazi diatribes. Conservatives see no reason why a learning tool of the journalism class should be permitted to become the instrument of a savage vendetta by one student who happens to be editor.

That is the conservative argument for censorship. The liberal position against censorship is based on the premises that high school students are almost adults and that political rights should extend inside the schools. The recognition that adolescents are in many respects adults is by no means modern, for in the Middle Ages youths 13 to 15 years old were treated as adults by society.[6] Students also were treated as adults as soon as they left home to attend school, and student conduct was regulated primarily by very democratic student governments. This relative freedom disappeared with the Renaissance, as educators developed the notions of the frailty of childhood and the moral responsibility of the masters to raise their charges properly.[7] Self-government disappeared and corporal punishment replaced fines as masters asserted themselves.[8] This is the authoritarian legacy inherited by the American educational system.

In the United States the liberal position emerged only in the 20th century, in large part under the influence of John Dewey. Although Dewey's focus was not specifically student rights, his arguments provided a philosophical base upon which claims for student rights could grow. Dewey stressed that learning should be dynamic, able to cope with change, and that an education should be an intellectual process of exploration by each student. With Dewey, the individual student eclipsed the teacher as the focal point of the educational process, and the scope of an education came to be conceived in far broader terms than before, encompassing preparation for a role in a democracy as well as the three R's.[9]

Dewey's writings subverted some of the time-honored precepts of the conservatives. Teachers no longer were seen as the guardians of all truth, and society began to recognize the intellect and activism--and sometimes the rights--of individual students. By presenting students as active and self-motivating, Dewey conceived of students in adult, rather than child-like, terms.

---

6. Philippe Aries, *Centuries of Childhood,* Robert Baldick, trans. (New York: Alfred ·A. Knopf, 1962), p. 154.
7. *Ibid.,* p. 253.
8. *Ibid.,* p. 258ff.
9. See John Dewey, *Democracy and Education* (New York: Macmillan Co., 1924).

And by emphasizing the relationship of the educational system to society and government, he laid the groundwork for arguments that rights should extend to the schools.

The liberal perspective borrows from Dewey first in emphasizing the maturity of students. Most high school editors are 18 years old by the time they graduate--old enough to drive, vote, marry, sign a contract, hold political office or go to war. The age of adulthood has dropped in a rapid-paced world in which young people are faced with many complex responsibilities. As long as they are given these responsibilities and as long as society makes demands of them, they should be permitted to express themselves politically. If students vote, they should be able to discuss for whom to vote. If they are drafted, they should be able to discuss the merits of the draft. In short, in a democratic society demands should not be made of people without giving them the opportunity to discuss the issues and seek redress.

High school students may need guidance and advice, but these should not be disguises for intimidation and coercion. A school newspaper adviser may advise, but the advice should not be binding. While there are dangers in entrusting the power of the press to young, inexperienced journalists, the solution is not to snatch the key to the press. "Some degree of abuse is inseperable from the proper use of every thing," James Madison wrote, "and in no instance is this more true than in that of the press." He continued: "It is better to leave a few of its noxious branches to their luxurient growth, than, by pruning them away, to injure the vigour of those yielding the proper fruits."[10]

While some high school editors certainly have abused their right of free press,[11] on the whole they seem to have behaved very responsibly. Reports of extreme sensationalism or vituperative attacks are rare and seem to occur more often in underground newspapers than in official school publications. The survey for this

10. James Madison, Report on the Virginia Resolutions (1799), *The Writings of James Madison,* Gaillard Hunt, ed. (New York: G.P. Putnam's Sons, 1906), Vol. VI, p. 389.
11. See "Report Card" section of *Student Press Law Center Report,* Vol. II, No. 3 (Fall, 1979) and subsequent issues.

book confirmed that most high school editors would make few changes in their newspapers even if they were not censored, and many exhibited a strong deference that suggests they would avoid any semblance of sensationalism. In sum, there seems to be little greater risk of irresponsible high school journalism than there is of irresponsible professional journalism--as illustrated each week by the *National Enquirer* and its ilk.

Liberals also protest the dichotomy between rights in society and rights in school. Stressing the interrelationship between a society and its educational system, liberals argue that schools should give students freedoms so they can learn to function in a democratic society. Moreover, any order in the schools that comes at the price of student rights is artificially imposed and stifles initiative and creativity. Suppressing criticism will not solve the problems--indeed, the American tradition has been that political disputes are best resolved through open debate.

It also is a mistake to believe that freedom of expression will always conflict with order. Only very rarely does a high school newspaper raise an issue so important and so immediate that it distracts the students from their studies. In those rare cases, the issue probably is important enough that it should be discussed, and the distraction probably will be profitable for the students, if only in the sense of encouraging awareness of pressing social and political issues. In fact, censorship in some cases is the greatest threat to order, because the conflicts it engenders spill over to the classrooms and distract students.

Liberals distinguish school newspapers from other teaching tools because the newspaper becomes a forum for ideas--and a democratic institution--in a way that an English class or biology experiment cannot. Newspapers contain ideas and promote discussion, while other classes are concerned for the most part with objective facts. A school should not permit a biology student to practice medicine because that is a skill that comes only through technical training. No person or sector of society has a monopoly on truth, however, so a student journalist may have something to contribute. According to John Stuart Mill's classic analysis, members of society always lose from censorship:

If the opinion is right, they are deprived of the opportunity of exchanging error for truth; if wrong, they lose, what is almost as great a benefit, the clearer perception and livelier impression of truth, produced by its collision with error.[12]

Whether one relies on Mill's utilitarian justification for freedom of expression or on the concept of free expression as a natural right, it seems this freedom should extend into the schools. Liberty of expression should apply not only to issues that are distant or national in scope, but also to those that are local--those that a student has the greatest chance of affecting. It would be absurd if a student could criticize his Congressman but not his principal, if he could protest draft registration but not his school's attendance policy.

The conservative argument that schools should screen newspapers for copy that would violate community standards also is untenable. Unless there is some compelling reason to distinguish rights in schools from rights in society, accepting this argument means that communities also should silence speakers or newspapers that offend local standards. On the contrary, liberal theory--and legal theory since about the 1960's--has stated that the offensiveness or outrageousness of political speech is an insufficient reason to prohibit its expression. Freedom of the press is important precisely because it applies to that with which we disagree vehemently; it would be trivial otherwise.

In granting freedom to the student newspaper, one must take the risk that the editor will offend the community, for protection of the sensibilities of the community is not a ground for censoring political speech.[13] A student newspaper editor should have as much right to crusade for Naziism or racism as any commercial newspaper editor or any private citizen. That the newspaper is publicly funded makes no difference: Citizens all the time pay taxes for causes

---

12. John Stuart Mill, *On Liberty*, in *The Utilitarians* (Garden City, N.Y.: Dolphin Books, 1961), p. 491.
13. "Political speech" here is used in the broadest sense, encompassing any discussion of government activities including school policies. However, political speech obviously would not embrace obscenity or libel.

they deplore--from welfare to military spending. Public bulletin boards may be used by protestors, or demonstrators may require expensive police protection from a hostile audience. Citizens make the initial decision about whether to have school newspapers, or public bulletin boards, or police, but once they have established them they cannot use the power of the purse to regulate what is discussed.

Of course, it is very unlikely that a student newspaper would embark upon an extremist political crusade, just as it is unlikely that a commercial newspaper editor would do so. Furthermore, it would be a good idea for a school newspaper to establish an editorial policy that requires the support of several editors for an editorial to be printed or a policy to be changed. That is simply sensible management and good journalism.

The conservative objection that principals and school boards should not be liable for obscene material that they cannot censor is valid, but the solution does not lie in limiting freedom of the press. The student editors and the publication itself should be liable, placing responsibility where it belongs, and school staff should be exempt precisely because they should have no authority over the content of the newspaper. While it is true that a plaintiff probably could not collect much from a few students and the school newspaper, the same is true of many small-town commercial newspapers. Certainly one should not limit freedom of expression for poor citizens or poor newspapers because they cannot pay hefty slander or libel judgments. In any event, the chances of a calamity such as libel or obscenity are extremely slim--the research for this book turned up no libel judgements against high school newspapers and only one instance where a judge found the content of a high school newspaper obscene.[14]

---

14. Another common conservative argument is that a high school principal is analogous to the publisher of a private newspaper, and therefore that he has a responsibility to regulate the content of the newspaper. However, this is primarily a legal argument, as even if the principal were in a position of publisher, the liberal arguments would hold that he should voluntarily cede his authority to the student editors. Therefore, the statement

According to this analysis, the conservative arguments seem bankrupt. High school students are not children. In today's fast-paced society, they are both aware and independent. Society judges them old enough to vote, to hold political office and to go to war. It would be ludicrous if they were then considered too immature to hold and express opinions. So long as high school students are considered old enough to have a right of freedom of expression, that right should accompany them in all circumstances.[15] Schools should not be closed societies where freedoms vanish,   for there is no reason to exclude students from the blanket of constitutional protections. Freedom of the press poses little threat to efficiency and order in schools; the only order it threatens is the contrived and superficial quiet that stifles free thought. Students will not learn less if their newspapers are freed, and they may learn something of how to function in a pluralistic, tolerant society.

Thus I believe that freedom of the press should extend into high schools, and that student press rights should be co-extensive with those of adult journalists. Certainly there should be restrictions on what the students may publish, and there are: Criminal and civil penalties exist for libel, invasions of privacy, copyright infringements and obscenity. Certainly there will be abuses of the power of the press by high school students, but as in the commercial press they will be outweighed by the benefits of freedom.

While full rights of freedom of the press seem appropriate for high school students, the same is not true of younger pupils. The first assumption--that the students are more adults than children--at some point is no longer valid, and it would be difficult to argue that even elementary school youngsters should be granted rights coextensive with those of the professional media. For the same reasons--most notably, lack of maturity--that elementary school children are not permitted to drive, to vote or to sign contracts, they probably should be constrained somewhat in their

---

that a principal acts as publisher will be evaluated with the legal arguments in Chapter IV.
15. Of course, this does not mean they could shout obscenities in the middle of class, any more than they could shout fire in a crowded theater. Such expressions are not political and are not protected.

publishing enterprises. They still should be allowed to criticize or comment on the school and on national and local governments, but prior restraint should be permitted so that an adviser may screen for libel or personal attacks against a student or teacher. Elementary school students, because of their lack of maturity and experience, would be more prone to such abuses than older students.[16]

Such a two-tiered system is not hypocritical, for the different treatment reflects real difference between high school and younger students. Paternalism for children is ingrained in society and aims to guide the children to a level of experience and maturity that will allow them to be responsible citizens, even responsible high school journalists. Such an enlightened paternalism is based on respect for the rights of children--their right to comment on school policies, for example--yet it also recognizes that the child's best interests sometimes are served by restraining him from an impetuous act.[17] The interests of neither the child nor the school community would be served, for example, by a child writing, "I hate Miss Jones" throughout the school newspaper during a temper tantrum. This is not political speech, and an adviser should be permitted to screen for such non-political and offensive remarks before publication.

My proposal, therefore, is that rights should increase with maturity. Political speech should be protected at all levels, but in elementary school and junior high school advisers should be empowered to review material before publication and screen for libel, obscenity, invasions of privacy, or personal attacks.[18] Such a two-tiered system would protect the

---

16. Edward T. Ladd argues that rights should be "stairstepped" as children get older, so that pupils get more and more rights as they rise from the category of "younger children" (aged 6 to 9) to "older children" (aged 10 to 13) to "youths" (aged 14 to 17) to adults (aged 18 and older). "Civil Liberties for Students--At What Age?" *Journal of Law and Education*, Vol. 3, No. 2 (April 1974), pp. 251-266.
17. See Amy Gutmann, "Children, Paternalism, and Education: A Liberal Argument," *Philosophy & Public Affairs*, Vol. 9, No. 4 (Summer 1980), pp. 338-58.
18. Of course, I recognize that most elementary school publications are far more likely to include awkward

right of all students to comment on and criticize the injustices they encounter in their schools, but at the elementary and junior high levels it would protect the school and the students themselves from any intemperate non-political speech. At the high school level, students would be free to write what they wished--and this freedom might breathe new life and spirit into high school newspapers.

---

short stories or attempts at verse than critical analyses of school policies or presidential politics. The right to examine substantive issues should exist, nonetheless.

IV

Censorship and the Law

For more than 120 years high school students have claimed a legal right of free expression, but for most of that time they were spurned by the courts. Only in 1969, in *Tinker v. Des Moines School District*, did the Supreme Court assert that high school students are "persons" within the meaning of the Constitution, whose rights extend into the classroom.[1] Even then the court left a gaping hole in the blanket of First Amendment protections, for the justices said expression could be censored if it were particularly disruptive. Just as in the previous chapter I argued that for social and educational reasons complete freedom of the press should extend into the high schools, here I will make the same argument from a legal perspective. I will argue that *Tinker* and its progeny are legally flawed and that under the First and Fourteenth Amendments--and a body of precedent--freedom of the press for public high school students should be coextensive with that of the professional news media.

The first known court case in the United States concerning freedom of expression for public school students is *Lander v. Seaver*,[2] dating from 1859 and typical of the early cases. An 11-year-old student had referred to his school master as "old Jack Seaver" while walking with some friends after school in front of the schoolmaster's house. The school master overheard the remark and whipped the student at school the next day. The student sued, and the Vermont Superior Court ruled for the schoolmaster, reasoning that the student's comment had "a direct and immediate

---

1. 393 U.S. 503 (1969).
2. 32 Vt. 114 (1859).

49

tendency to injure the school, to subvert the master's authority, and to beget disorder and insubordination."[3] The court continued:

All such or similar acts tend to impair the usefulness of the school, the welfare of the scholars and the authority of the master. By Common consent and by the universal custom in our New England schools, the master has always been deemed to have the right to punish such offenses. Such power is essential to the preservation of order, decency, decorum and good government in the schools.[4]

This ruling, so clearly a part of the conservative authoritarian tradition discussed in Chapter III, emphasized two legal doctrines that were relied upon in similar cases for most of the next century. The first was *in loco parentis,* the notion that the parent cedes to the school some of the parental authority over the child. The second doctrine was minimum scrutiny for student rights cases, placing the burden of proof on the student to show that his constitutional rights had been violated.[5] These doctrines were incorporated into later court rulings that upheld the expulsion of a student whose mother criticized a teacher in front of a class,[6] the expulsion of two high school students who wrote a poem satirizing school rules that was published in a town newspaper,[7] and the expulsion of a student who criticized school rules in a speech to the student body.[8]

---

3. 32 Vt. at 120.
4. 32 Vt. at 121.
5. Minimum scrutiny assumed that courts should intervene only to prohibit *ultra vires* actions--those clearly beyond the scope of school authority. Other school policies and actions, those reasonable or at least not arbitrary, were permitted to stand.
6. Board of Education v. Purse, 101 Ga. 422, 28 S.E. 896 (1897).
7. State ex. re. Dresser v. District Board, 135 Wis. 619, 116 N.W. 232 (1908).
8. Wooster v. Sunderland, 27 Cal. App. 51 (1915). See also Wilson v. Abilene Independent School District, 190 S.W. 2d 406 (Texas Ct. of Appeals, 1945), Pugsley v. Sellmeyer, 158 Ark. 247, 250 S.W. 538 (1923).

The few commentators who have taken the trouble to look for the ancestors of recent decisions like *Tinker* usually have found a liberal strain emerging only in the 1940's and 50's.[9] Actually the liberal strain, although muted, dates from much earlier. Even the first case, *Lander v. Seaver*, expressed some concern for the students' right of expression, and an 1870 decision in Iowa overturned the expulsion of a student who had written two articles in a political journal criticizing his school board.[10] As early as 1923, in *Meyer v. Nebraska*,[11] the Supreme Court recognized a Fourteenth Amendment right of students to acquire knowledge. The court, relying on the doctrine of substantive due process then in vogue, used a reasonable relation test to strike down a state statute prohibiting the teaching of foreign languages to children. The pupils' right to acquire knowledge was only one among many rights (of teachers and parents) the court found the statute to violate. Two years later, in *Pierce v. Society of Sisters*,[12] the court also restricted the educational authority of the state, but in *Pierce* it relied exclusively upon the rights of parents without considering the rights of students.

Freedom of expression was explicitly extended into the schools in 1943, in *West Virginia State Board of Education v. Barnette*.[13] A majority of the justices ruled in this case that students have a First Amendment right not to salute the American flag. Eleven years later, in *Brown v. Board of Education*,[14] the Supreme Court focused on the rights of students in finding that segregated schooling violated the equal protection clause of the Fourteenth Amendment.[15] Together, these cases show that the courts were chipping away at the

---

9. See, for example, Carol L. Ziegler, *Struggle in the Schools: Constitutional Protection for Public High School Students*, (Princeton University: Woodrow Wilson Association Monograph Series in Public Affairs No. 1, 1970), and Jill H. Krafte, "Tinker's Legacy: Freedom of the Press in Public High Schools," *DePaul Law Review*, Vol. 28 (Winter 1979), pp. 387-428.
10. Murphy v. Board of Directors of Marengo District, 30 Iowa 429 (1870).
11. 262 U.S. 390 (1923).
12. 268 U.S. 510 (1925).
13. 319 U.S. 624 (1943). Cf. Prince v. Massachusetts, 321 U.S. 158 (1944).
14. 347 U.S. 483 (1954).

traditional, conservative approach to education well before the explosion of legally-mandated student rights under the Warren Court.

The first great expansion of the legal rights of young people under the Warren court came in *In Re Gault,* [16] a 1967 decision that due process protections for criminal defendants generally must apply to the juvenile justice system. On behalf of the majority, Justice Fortas wrote: "Whatever may be their precise impact, neither the Fourteenth Amendment nor the Bill of Rights is for adults alone.... Under our Constitution, the condition of being a boy does not justify a kangaroo court."[17]

The second great explosion of rights for young people was *Tinker v. Des Moines Independent School District,* [18] the landmark case in 1969 that unequivocally extended First Amendment rights of expression to public high school students. The case arose in December 1965, when John F. Tinker, a 15-year-old high school junior, his sister Mary Beth Tinker, a 13-year-old junior high student, and Christopher Eckhardt, a 16-year-old high school junior, decided to wear black armbands to school to protest the Vietnam War. The principals of the Des Moines schools heard of the plan and adopted a rule that armbands could not be worn in school. The three were suspended when they refused to take them off.

The students sued and lost at the District Court and Appellate Court level. Writing for the majority of the Supreme Court, Justice Fortas reversed the lower court decisions and ruled that the students had a Constitutional right of free expression within the schools:

---

15. A companion case for the District of Columbia, Bolling v. Sharpe, 347 U.S. 497 (1954), found that segregation in Washington, D.C., violated the students' right to liberty under the Fifth Amendment due process clause. The court had to use the weaker Fifth Amendment argument because the Fourteenth Amendment applies only to the states and not to Washington, D.C.
16. 387 U.S. 1 (1967).
17. 387 U.S. at 13, 28.
18. 393 U.S. 503 (1969).

First Amendment rights, applied in light of the special characteristics of the school environment, are available to teachers and students. It can hardly be argued that either students or teachers shed their constitutional rights to freedom of speech or expression at the schoolhouse gate....

In our system, state-operated schools may not be enclaves of totalitarianism. School officials do not possess absolute authority over their students. Students in school as well as out of school are "persons" under our Constitution. They are possessed of fundamental rights which the state must respect, just as they themselves must respect their obligations to the State.[19]

Justice Fortas employed strict scrutiny and in this case found no compelling state interest to justify prohibition of expression. But this finding was based on the facts of the case--that no significant disruption had occurred at the schools--and the court expressly stated that expression need not be tolerated where "school authorities...forecast substantial or material interference with school activities."[20] While some observers argue that *Tinker* liberated high school journalists and placed them almost on an equal footing with professional journalists, clearly this is not so.

Fortas affirmed the "comprehensive authority of the States and of school officials...to prescribe and control conduct in schools."[21] He cited the "special characteristics of the school environment,"[22] and

---

19. 393 U.S. at 506, 511. Justice Black dissented vigorously, arguing that the court was overstepping its bounds in regulating schools and that freedom of expression would divert students' attention from their schoolwork. He wrote: "If the day has come when pupils of state-supported schools, kindergartens, grammar schools, or high schools, can defy and flout orders of school officials to keep their minds on their own schoolwork, it is the beginning of a new revolutionary era of permissiveness in this country fostered by the judiciary." 393 U.S. at 518.
20. 393 U.S. at 514. This test was first developed in Burnside v. Byars, 363 F.2d 744, 749 (5th Cir. 1966).
21. 393 U.S. at 507.

approved of censorship to prevent substantial disruption. If the Des Moines principal had had a good reason to forecast a significant disruption because of the armbands, the court would have approved of the suspensions. Fortas also stressed that the armbands, as a quiet, peaceful, political expression were almost "pure speech" and thus entitled to special protection.[23] Two weeks after the *Tinker* decision, Fortas concurred in a denial of certiorari in a similar case because the expression was less than pure.[24] *Tinker* should be seen as an enormous advance for public high school students, but it did not go so far as to grant rights coextensive with those of adult society.

Tinker did not mention freedom of the press for high school journalists, but it provided the philosophical justification for lower courts to extend the "substantial disruption" test to expression in school newspapers. In essence, *Tinker* viewed the school as a public forum where expression must be tolerated. According to forum theory, once the government opens a public forum--be it a park, street, plaza or school--it cannot regulate the debate therein, unless the debate threatens the primary purpose of the forum.[25] The lower courts applied forum theory to school newspapers, ruling that advisers and administrators may censor only copy that is libelous, obscene or "materially and substantially" disruptive of school operations.[26]

---

22. 393 U.S. at 506.
23. 393 U.S. at 505.
24. Barker v. Hardway, 394 U.S. 905 (1969), *cert. denied.*
25. Even when the debate threatens the forum's primary purpose, the debate may not be constrained unless the constraints are applied fairly to all and are narrowly spelled out in the statutes. Edwards v. South Carolina, 372 U.S. 229 (1963); Gregory v. Chicago, 394 U.S. 111 (1969); Cox v. Louisiana [Cox I], 379 U.S. 536 (1965).
26. Although the courts have universally accepted application of the Tinker standard to high school newspapers, the Attorney General of Oregon rejected this interpretation in a 1978 advisory opinion. Attorney General James A. Redden, now a federal judge, reasoned that the school district is analogous to the publisher of a private newspaper and therefore has final control over the newspaper. "Just as the owner of a private

The lower courts have handed down far too many cases since *Tinker* to examine each individually, so the case law will be presented here by topic. The following areas will be examined: underground newspapers; junior high schools; criticism of school officials; obscenity; libel; prior restraint; confidential sources; private schools; and indirect censorship.[27]

Underground Newspapers

The courts have clearly established that students have a right to publish and distribute underground newspapers, subject to the same restrictions of libel, obscenity and substantial disruption--as well as those of time, place and manner of distribution--that exist for official publications. Because the school is a public forum, the right to self-expression is protected regardless of whether the expression appears in an official or unofficial newspaper.[28]

---

newspaper can dictate policy to an employee, the editor, so can a school district dictate policy to the editor it has chosen for its newspaper." Opinion No. 7630, p. 4. See also Opinion No. 7735. The Attorney General could cite no cases to support his position, and his argument is contradicted by every tenet of forum theory. Because the school is a government-sponsored forum, the content of the debate may not be regulated. If a school principal were analogous to a private publisher, so too a city parks department would be analogous to the caretaker of a private park and could exclude anyone at will. But public parks and public schools are very different from their private counterparts and expression may not be curtailed in such public places merely at the whim of the manager of the forum.

27. In addition to court rulings extending freedom of expression to public high schools, the California State Legislature in 1977 approved a law recognizing the right of public school students to engage in political expression. The statute (Cal. Educ. Code Sec. 48916) permits censorship and prior restraint only of material that is obscene or libelous, or that incites unlawful acts or leads to substantial disruption.

28. Bright v. Los Angeles School District, 134 Cal. Rep. 639, 556 P.2d 1081 (1976); Fujishama v. Board

Junior High Schools

Only two cases are known that applied directly to junior high school students, and both rulings suggest that junior high school students have the same rights as senior high school students. *Tinker* itself is relevant because one of the petitioners, Mary Beth Tinker, was a 13-year-old eighth grader attending junior high school. Nowhere did the court distinguish between her rights and those of her brother, who was in senior high school. Likewise, the only other case to arise from a junior high setting upheld the students' rights and did not suggest that they had any fewer rights than senior high students.[29] While the courts could set more stringent standards for obscenity in junior high publications, that issue has not been litigated.

Criticism of School Officials

The courts have interpreted the "substantial disruption" test strictly, protecting the most bitter attacks on school officials so long as the attacks do not disrupt the school. The Seventh Circuit Court of Appeals, for example, upheld a high school editor's right to characterize his senior dean's comments as "the product of a sick mind."[30] The editor also termed the attendance policy "utterly idiotic and asinine" and urged students to destroy "propaganda" given them by the school to take home to their parents.[31]

---

of Education, 460 F.2 1355 (7th Cir. 1972); Jacobs v. Board of School Commissioners, 490 F.2d 601 (7th Cir. 1973); Nitzberg v. Parks, 525 F.2d 378 (4th Cir. 1975); Poxon v. Board of Education, 341 F. Supp. 256 (E.D. Cal. 1971); Riseman v. School Committee of City of Quincy, 439 F.2d 148 (1st Cir. 1971; Scoville v. Board of Education of Joliet Township, 425 F.2d 10 (7th Cir. 1970); Shanley v. Northeast Independent School District, 462 F.2d 960 (5th Cir. 1972); Thomas v. Board of Education, 607 F.2d 1043 (2nd Cir. 1979); Vail v. Board of Education, 354 F. Supp. 592 (D.N.H. 1973).

29. Riseman v. School Committee of the City of Quincy, 439 F.2d 148 (1st Cir. 1971).

30. Scoville v. Board of Education, 425 F.2d 10, 16 (7th Cir. 1970).

31. 425 F.2d at 16.

One instance where censorship was upheld was a principal's seizure of a school newspaper because of two letters to the editor it contained. The first letter was from the lacrosse team complaining in ungentlemanly terms about sports coverage and drawing an equally ungentlemanly retort from the sports editor. The second letter criticized the student body vice president for "total failure in performing his duties" and labeled him a "disgrace to the school." The letter also said the student body vice president had been suspended from school and had cheated by changing his grades in school records. The principal justified seizure of the newspapers by claiming that publication of the first letter would result in a fight between lacrosse players and the sports editor and that the second letter was inaccurate and possibly libelous. The court accepted the principal's arguments and ruled that the censorship was permissible to avoid substantial disruption of the school.[32] Other courts have upheld the punishment of pupils for "flagrant and defiant disobedience of the school authorities," even when their expression itself is protected.[33]

Obscenity

The Supreme Court has held that obscenity is not protected by the First Amendment, but the court has defined obscenity strictly enough so that only sexually-explicit pornography may be prohibited as obscene.[34] Although the Supreme Court has ruled that states may set a standard of obscenity for minors

---

32. Frasca v. Andrew, 463 F. Supp. 1043 (E.D.N.Y. 1978). Quotes are from "Judge Upholds Newspaper Seizure," *Student Press Law Center Report,* Vol. II, No. 1 (Winter 1978-79), p. 25.
33. Schwartz v. Schuker, 298 F. Supp. 238, 241 (E.D.N.Y. 1969); Sullivan V. Houston Independent School District, 475 F. 2d 1071 (5th Cir. 1973), *cert. denied,* 414 U.S. 1032 (1973).
34. Roth v. United States, 354 U.S. 476 (1957); Miller v. California, 413 U.S. 15 (1973). The test for obscenity involves three findings: first, that the average person, using local standards, would find the overall tone of the work appealing to the prurient interest; second, that the work depicts patently offensive sexual conduct; and third, that the work lacks serious literary, artistic, political or scientific value. 413 U.S. at 24.

different from that of adults,[35] the lower courts for the most part have refused to accept the claims of high school administrators that four-letter words in school newspapers constitute obscenity and may be censored. Typically, the newspapers contain four-letter words in fiery political editorials or in quotations used in articles. With only one exception, the courts have ruled that four-letter words and other vulgarities do not constitute obscenity and may not be censored.[36]

The one exception was a 1969 U.S. District Court decision (handed down nine months after *Tinker*) approving the suspension of high school students who distributed an underground newspaper that contained four-letter words in an article entitled "The Student as Nigger," as well as a retouched photo of President Nixon with his middle finger extended.[37] Not only does this finding contradict every other court decision on the subject, but it seems at odds with the conceptual framework established by the Supreme Court for obscenity cases. The court has taken great pains to stress that obscenity refers only to explicit sexual material and not to political expression.[38] A 1975 opinion stated that even for minors not all nudity may be regulated as obscene,[39] and in all cases the court has stressed that obscenity is confined to the erotic. The Supreme Court specifically ruled that four-letter words—and a political cartoon of a policeman raping the Statue of Liberty—are not obscene in college publications,[40] although the same standards do not

35. Ginsberg v. New York, 390 U.S. 629 (1968).
36. Jacobs v. Board of School Commissioners, 490 F.2d 601 (7th Cir. 1973), *dismissed as moot,* 420 U.S. 128 (1975); Koppell v. Levine, 347 F. Supp. 456 (E.D.N.Y. 1972); Thomas v. Board of Education, 707 F.2d 1043 (2d Cir. 1979); Vail v. Board of Education, 354 F. Supp. 592 D.N.H. 1973; Vought v. Van Buren Public School, 306 F. Supp. 1388 (E.D. Mich. 1969).
37. The photo appeared above the caption, "Here's a Little Something for You Justice." Baker v. Downey City Board of Education, 307 F. Supp. 517.
38. Roth V. United States, 354 U.S. 476 (1957); Miller v. California, 413 U.S. 15 (1973); Cohen v. California, 403 U.S. 15 (1971).
39. Erznoznik v. City of Jacksonville, 422 U.S. 205, 213 (1975).
40. Papish v. Board of Curators of the University of Missouri, 410 U.S. 667 (1973).

necessarily apply to high school newspapers as to college publications.[41] Even if the same standards do not apply, it seems entirely inappropriate to classify four-letter words and a retouched photo as obscene. These may shock, these may be in poor taste, but so long as they are not erotic it is difficult to understand how they could be considered legally obscene. Instead, four-letter words and other vulgarities should be evaluated by the substantial disruption test, which surely would protect them. Most high school students probably find four-letter words less startling than the four-syllable words they encounter in English class.

Libel

Unlike obscenity, there is no reason to establish different standards for minors and adults in libel cases; therefore the same definitions of libel exist for high school papers as for commercial newspapers. Because libel standards for public figures are quite rigorous and because high school publications traditionally have avoided controversy, there have been very few libel suits against schools or student editors. At least one court has ruled that student body officers are public figures for libel purposes;[42] if this doctrine becomes generally accepted, school newspapers will find it much easier to comment on school controversies without risking libel. The research for this book turned up no successful libel suits against school newspapers, although there has been at least one judgment (and several out-of-court settlements) against a high school yearbook.[43]

---

41. See Quarterman v. Byrd, 453 F.2d 54 (4th Cir. 1971); Schwartz v. Schuker, 298 F. Supp. 238 (E.D.N.Y. 1969); Katz v. McAulay, 438 F.2d 1058 (2nd Cir. 1971); Koppell v. Levine, 347 F. Supp. 456 (E.D.N.Y. 1972). See also Ginsberg v. New York, 390 U.S. 629 (1968).
42. Henderson v. Van Buren Public School, 4 Med. L. Rep. 1741 (Summary Judgement E.D. Mich. 1978). Public figures must prove malice, instead of just negligence, to win a libel suit.
43. Yearbooks have been vulnerable to libel suits because of the practice of putting quotations or statements under student photographs. One student won a $38,000 judgement when the double-entendre, "A good fisherman and a master baiter," appeared

In the few libel cases that have arisen out of high school publications, the school usually has been liable for damages.[44] This liability, though not firmly established because of the dearth of cases, has led school administrators to argue that they should have a right to prior restraint, not just of articles clearly libelous but also of any that conceivably might provoke an expensive lawsuit. That logic is understandable, for if school officials are liable for damages they should be in a position to prevent the libel. Just the defense costs in a libel suit may be substantial, so administrators could make a strong agrument that before they skimp on books or teacher salaries, they should censor controversial articles to reduce the risk of expensive lawsuits.

Such an approach, however, would chill freedom of the press in high schools and would contravene the spirit of *Tinker* and subsequent cases. A better solution to the problem lies in redefining liability so that school officials are not liable for the iniquities of student editors. In some states, schools are now immune from libel suits under the doctrine of sovereign immunity, which holds that state institutions of learning are not liable for the torts of their employees. Sovereign immunity is applicable only in certain states, however, so a proposal to change liability requires a broader legal justification.

In those few cases that have arisen, school boards have been liable under the theory of vicarious liablity. According to this doctrine, a business is liable for the actions of its employees and agents. Vicarious liability hinges on the control the owner has over his agents, and whether the wrong occurs in the course of employment, so if school officials are not permitted to censor articles they should not be subject to liability.[45]

---

under his photograph in the yearbook. Mele v. Cuddy, Essex County Court, Newark, N.J. (1970). See also George E. Stevens and John B. Webster, *Law and the Student Press* (Ames, Iowa: Iowa State Univ. Press, 1973), Chapter II.

44. Mele v. Cuddy, Essex County Court, Newark, N.J. (1970); out-of-court settlements by school boards and principals discussed in Stevens and Webster, pp. 40-52.

If liability no longer extended to school boards and principals under vicarious liability, the students themselves would be liable, for they are the ones writing and editing the articles. The student's parents would not be liable unless they were familiar with the libel or had failed to control their children. Of course, few students would be in a position to pay much in damages, but they would feel the responsibility for all that they wrote. The penury of the students is not a valid argument against making them solely liable for what they write, for that argument implies that citizens should have to post collateral before expressing themselves. Poor persons occasionally may defame other people, but this is not a sufficient reason to prevent poor people from speaking--or from publishing newspapers.[46]

Prior Restraint

While the courts have agreed that school officials may restrict articles that are libelous, obscene or very disruptive, there is no consensus as to what form the restrictions may take. The *Tinker* decision did not discuss prior restrains--generally defined as any interference with a newspaper before it is distributed --and it has been left to the lower courts to decide whether school officials can censor articles beforehand, or whether they must wait until the newspaper is distributed and then punish the editor. Prior restraints obviously are more effective, in that by the time the newspaper is distributed it may be too late to prevent the libel or disruption. However, the Supreme Court has been very wary of prior restraints because they choke the circulation of ideas before appeals and

---

45. Similar arguments hold for distributor's liability, which also might apply to school administrators. See Christopher B. Fager, *Ownership and Control of the Student Press: A First Amendment Analysis* (Washington, D.C.: Student Press Law Center, mimeo), pp. 35-36.
46. It should be stressed that libel is a very slight risk. No school is known to have lost a libel suit relating to its student newspaper, and Prosser lists only three cases in which minors were found liable for defamation. The last of those three cases occured in 1910. William L. Prosser, *Handbook of the Law of Torts*, 4th ed. (St. Paul, Minn.: West Publishing Co., 1971), p. 997, n. 75.

procedural protections are exhausted. In adult society, prior restraints are acceptable only for obscenity in films and perhaps for extreme cases involving national security.[47] Only the Seventh Circuit Court of Appeals has flatly ruled that any system of prior restraint in a high school newspaper is unconstitutional,[48] although other circuit courts have invalidated specific prior review policies for lack of procedural safeguards. The First Circuit also has hinted that prior restraints are unconstitutional *per se* [49] and two U.S. District Courts have rejected prior restraints on broad grounds.[50] Even the Seventh Circuit ruling that prior restraints are unconstitutional *per se* may be in doubt, for in a later decision the same circuit rejected a system of prior restraint on the basis of overbreadth and vagueness.[51] That should have been unnecessary if all systems of prior restraint were unconstitutional on their face.

While most of the appellate courts have declined to declare prior restraints unconstitutional *per se,* in all but two cases they upheld the students by rejecting the specific system of prior restraint in question. Only as dicta did they suggest they might approve a more precisely-drawn plan for prior restraint.[52] The two exceptions are recent and do not deal directly with

47. Times Film Corp. v. Chicago, 365 U.S. 43 (1961); United States v. Progressive, 467 F. Supp. 990 (W.D. Wisc. 1979). See also Near v. Minnesota, 283 U.S. 697 (1931), and New York Times Co. v. United States, 403 U.S. 713 (1971).
48. Fujishama v. Board of Education, 460 F.2d 1355 (7th Cir. 1972).
49. Riseman v. School Committee of Quincy, 439 F.2d 148, 149 n. 2 (1st Cir. 1971).
50. The order in Vail v. Board of Education, 354 F. Supp. 592 (D.N.H. 1973), stated there would be no prior review; and the district court in Sullivan v. Houston Independent School District, 333 F. Supp. 1149 (S.D. Tex. 1971), rejected all prior restraints. However, the Sullivan decision was overturned by the circuit court, *supplemental injunctions vacated,* 475 F.2d 1071 (5th Cir. 1973).
51. Jacobs v. Board of School Commissioners, 490 F.2d 601 (7th Cir. 1973), *vacated as moot,* 420 U.S. 128 (1975).
52. Baughman v. Freienmuth, 478 F.2d 1345 (4th Cir. 1973); Eisner V. Stamford Board of Education, 440 F.2d 803 (2nd Cir. 1971); Nitzberg v. Parks, 525

the editorial content of the newspapers. In *Trachtman v. Anker* [53] the Second Circuit upheld a principal who refused to allow the staff of the newspaper to survey the sexual attitudes of students. The court upheld the prior restraint not on the basis of the substantial disruption test but on the ground that the survey would invade the rights of the students and cause them "significant emotional harm."[54] *Tinker* had included the caveat that student expression could not invade the rights of others, but this was the first time this justification was used for censorship. Because *Trachtman* applied to a request for information rather than to a newspaper, and because it relied on the peculiar "invasion of rights" test, the decision is not easily extended to other high school First Amendment cases. Nevertheless, it is significant because it marks the first time that a federal appellate court upheld a system of prior restraint.

The other decision to uphold prior restraint was handed down by the Fourth Circuit in June 1980.[55] It upheld a principal's seizure of an underground newspaper that contained an advertisement for drug paraphernalia. The court also found that a school rule forbidding literature that "encourages actions which endanger the health or safety of students" was not too vague.[56] This decision, too, may be distinguished from most cases because it dealt with an advertisement, but still it is clear that the courts--with the possible exception of the First and Seventh Circuits-- accept prior restraint of high school publications as constitutionally permissible.[57]

F.2d 378 (4th Cir. 1975); Quaterman v. Byrd, 453 F.2d 54 (4th Cir. 1971); Shanley v. Northeast Independent School District, 465 F.2d 960 (5th Cir. 1972).

53. 563 F.2d 512 (2d Cir. 1977), cert. denied, 435 U.S. 925 (1978).

54. 563 F.2d at 520.

55. Williams v. Spencer, 622 F.2d 1200 (4th Cir.1980).

56. 622 F.2d at 1203, 1205.

57. However, the circuits differ in the scrutiny they apply to prior restraints. The Fourth Circuit often has applied strict scrutiny, while the Second and Fifth Circuits have applied minimum scrutiny. Nitzberg v. Parks, 525 F.2d 378 (4th Cir. 1975); Gambino v. Fairfax County School Board, 429 F. Supp. 731 (E.D. Va. 1977), affirmed, 564 F.2d 157

Access to the News

As high school students gained new freedoms in what they might print, they began to expand their traditional horizons and imitate the professional news media. Just within the last few years, student editors have demanded the right to attend school board meetings and government news conferences. For the most part, the government still refuses to grant press credentials to the student press, but a few inroads have been made. The Arkansas State Police gave in to the threat of a lawsuit and began issuing press passes to high school and college journalists.[58] An Oregon school board settled out of court with a student editor and agreed to open almost all school board meeting to students.[59] The Oregon attorney general has ruled that a high school newspaper reporter is a "representative of the news media" under state law and therefore is entitled to attend executive sessions of school board meetings. However, through tortuous reasoning the attorney general concluded that school officials have control over student newspapers and therefore may prevent students from exercising their rights as representatives of the news media.[60]

Denying high school journalists credentials that routinely are given to their older colleagues may be discriminatory and unconstitutional under the equal protection clause of the Fourteenth Amendment. If students are denied access on the basis that only salaried or full-time reporters are given credentials, then the rules might stand. But in most cases students are denied credentials simply because they are students, and part-time or unsalaried reporters would be given credentials if they asked for them. In such cases, student journalist are being discriminated

---

(4th Cir. 1977); Eisner v. Stamford Board of Education, 440 F.2d 803 (2nd Cir. 1971); Shanley V. Northeast Independent School District, 462 F.2d 960 (5th Cir. 1972). The Fourth Circuit's continued use of strict scrutiny is uncertain after the Trachtman and Williams decisions.
58. "Students Win Press Accreditation," *Student Press Law Center Report*, Vol. II, No. 2 (Spring 1979),p. 5.
59. "Board Gives in to Suit: No Review, Meetings Open," *Student Press Law Center Report*, Vol. II, No. 3 (Fall 1979), p. 14.
60. Opinion No. 7735, March 16 1979. See note 26 above.

against, and such discrimination may violate their right to equal protection under the law.

Advertisements and Access to the Newspaper

The right of journalists--students and professional--to solicit and publish most kinds of advertising is firmly established, for the courts have ruled that "speech is not stripped of First Amendment protection merely because it appears in [advertisements]."[61] High school newspapers may carry most types of advertising, commercial or political,[62] but schools probably may ban advertisements that promote illicit activity, such as use of narcotics.[63] A related issue is whether high school editors must accept all political advertising and letters to the editor. Some commentators argue that high school newspapers--as public forums--have an obligation to provide equal access to all points of view, so that the editors may not reject political advertisements or letters to the editor.[64] The courts have not addressed this issue in a high school context, and at the college level the courts have responded differently. The Fourth Circuit indicated as dicta that "there are strong arguments" for mandatory equal access, while the Fifth Circuit rejected this argument and ruled that editors may reject political advertising.[65]

The Fifth Circuit's position is more persuasive. Rules mandating equal access are constraints as

61. Bigelow v. Virginia, 421 U.S. 809, 818 (1975).
62. Hernandez v. Hanson, 430 F. Supp. 1154 (D. Neb. 1973); Pliscou v. Holtville Unified School District, 411 F. supp. 842 (S.D. Cal. 1976); Zucker v. Panitz, 299 F. Supp. 102 (S.D.N.Y. 1969).
63. Williams v. Spencer, 622 F.2d 1200 (4th Cir.
64. See Forrest E. Claypool, "Note, Public Forum Theory in the Educational Setting: The First Amendment and the Student Press," *University of Illinois Law Forum*, Vol. 1979, No. 4, pp. 908-12; and Jerome A. Barron, *Freedom of the Press for Whom?* (Bloomington, Ind.: Indiana University Press, 1973), Chapter 3.
65. Joyner v. Whiting, 477 F.2d 456 (4th Cir. 1973) at 462; Mississippi Gay Alliance v. Goudelock, 536 F.2d 1073 (5th Cir. 1976).

insidious as rules prohibiting certain articles. The point of freedom of the press is to permit journalists almost-complete freedom in determining the newspaper's content, and to remove political discussions from the scrutiny of the government. It would be breathtaking indeed if the First Amendment ("Congress shall make no law...abridging the freedom of speech, or of the press") were interpreted to mean that high school newspapers must by law open their columns to outsiders.

The Supreme Court has ruled that no right of access exists for private newspapers,[66] and the same practical arguments against forced access in private papers exist for school newspapers. Almost everyone has strong beliefs about something, and it would be absurd to contend that a newspaper must provide expensive column space to anyone with strong opinions. Ultimately this is an effort to mandate a measure of responsibility in the press--through affirmative demands rather than negative constraints--yet the legal and historical tradition in the United States is that responsibility is nurtured best in an atmosphere of complete editorial freedom for newspapers.

Confidential Sources

Professional journalists first claimed a constitutional right to protect confidential sources in 1958,[67] and in the 1970's this area became a major battleground between the press and the courts. These claims arise less often in the high school setting because few high school newspapers are sufficiently aggressive to use unnamed sources in reporting illegal activity. In March 1981, however, there was such a case and it attracted widespread publicity, including an editorial and front page article in *The New York Times*. The case arose when *The Orange and Blue Tattler*, the newspaper of Millville Senior High School in Millville, N.J., published an interview by an unnamed reporter with "Candy Man," a drug dealer who said he sold marijuana to elementary school students and hard drugs to high school pupils. The county prosecutor subpoenaed the newspaper adviser to tell the grand jury who the student interviewer was, so that the student could be asked "Candy Man's" real name.

---

66. Miami Herald Publishing Co. v. Tornillo, 418 U.S. 241 (1974).
67. Garland v. Torre, 259 F.2d 545 (1958).

A Superior Court judge rejected the school's claims that the newspaper adviser and reporter were protected from orders to disclose confidential sources by the First Amendment and by New Jersey's "shield law." However, the judge told the prosecutor to wait a week and try to find out the name of the pusher through less confrontational means. On March 31 the grand jury withdrew the subpoena on the recommendation of the prosecutor, saying in a statement that "Candy Man" probably had stopped dealing or left the area because of the publicity.[68]

The judge had ruled that the shield law did not protect high school journalists because the newspaper did not meet the statute's requirements--the *Tattler* did not have a mailing permit, have paid circulation or print advertising. The judge said the First Amendment forbade interference with publication and distribution of newspapers, but permitted orders for journalists to testify to grand juries. In this respect the judge was following precedents established by the Supreme Court, which in 1972 ruled that a Louisville newspaper reporter could be compelled to testify to a grand jury about narcotics activity he had witnessed while researching several articles on the subject.[69] It appears student journalists will have the same difficulties as professional reporters in protecting their confidential sources, and students may have the added difficulty that they may not fit the news media definition in state shield laws.

Perhaps a more likely threat to the confidentiality of sources is that angry principals will demand that student reporters name the anonymous persons who criticize the school in articles in the newspaper. While this issue apparently has not been litigated, any such demands by a principal might be beyond the scope

---

68. Dierdre Carmody, "School Paper's Article on Drug Dealer Spurs Battle on Press Rights," *The New York Times,* March 26, 1981, p. 1; Donald Janson, "School Paper's Adviser Facing Court Order," *The New York Times,* March 27, 1981, p. B1; Donald Janson, "Jury Decides Not to Query Adviser to School's Paper," *The New York Times,* April 1, 1981, p. B2; and "'Candy Man' Went Thataway," editorial, *The New York Times,* April 4, 1981, p. 22.
69. Branzburg v. Hayes, 408 U.S. 665 (1972). See also New York Times Co. v. Jascalevich, 493 U.S. 1331 (1978), *cert. denied.*

of his authority. Therefore, even if they do not violate the students' First Amendment rights, they could be *ultra vires* --invalid because they are beyond the legitimate power of the schools and principals.

Private Schools

The First Amendment protects the citizen only from the government, and so it is generally thought not to apply to private schools. Disputes over censorship have arisen at private schools, but they have not been litigated and so the courts have not addressed this issue. One attorney has argued that First Amendment protections should extend to private school students, on the basis that private schools are fulfilling a public duty--prescribed by statue--and that the schools therefore should be subject to Constitutional restrictions.[70] The Supreme Court has indeed found state action in ostensibly private activities where there was state "involvement" or "authorization."[71] However, the court in other cases has stressed the rights of property owners to use their land as they wish. For example, the court ruled in 1972 that protesters do not have a right to distribute literature in a private shopping mall.[72]

An extraordinary leap of the imagination would be required to argue that private school--the distinguishing feature of which is that they are not state-run--are agents of the state and therefore must respect First Amendment rights. Indeed, such a finding might do away with parochial schools, for if the First Amendment mandated freedom of expression, it also would forbid religious education.

---

70. Jeffrey W. Kobrick, letter to Fontbonne Academy, in *Student Rights Litigation Packet* (Cambridge, Mass.: Harvard Center for Law and Education, 1972), pp. 83-84.
71. Shelly v. Kraemer, 334 U.S. 1 (1948); Burton v. Wilmington Parking Authority, 365 U.S. 715; Reitman v. Mulkey, 387 U.S. 369 (1967). These cases all involved racial discrimination, and the justices presumably would be less inclined to go out on a limb for the sake of newspaper editors at private high schools.
72. Lloyd Corp. v. Tanner, 407 U.S. 551 (1972). See also Jackson v. Metropolitan Edison Co., 419 U.S. 345 (1974).

Indirect Censorship

High school administrators bent on censorship have with practice become more sophisticated in their repression. Instead of openly censoring articles or expelling editors, they sometimes apply pressure on the adviser or threaten to cut off funds to the publication. Several advisers have been fired for refusing to censor, and some publications have been closed or suspended because they offended administrators. In the most blatant cases--where administrators acknowledge that their actions were motivated by displeasure with the newspaper's content--courts have reinstated advisers and restored funds to newspapers.[73] However, administrators usually are discreet enough to mask their real reasons behind accusations of poor job performance or tales of tight budgets. In these circumstances there is little or nothing that can be done. Community pressure may be more effective than the law in preventing such abuses by the administration.

Such is the state of the case law of freedom of the press for high school students. Clearly the courts have responded differently in applying *Tinker* to the high school press. One reason is that *Tinker* was marred by a deficiency from which the case law has not been able to recover.

The flaw of the *Tinker* decision is its improper use of forum theory to justify restrictions based on the content of the expression. Not only *Tinker* but other cases as well have determined that schools are public forums, and that "the classroom is peculiarly the 'marketplace of ideas.'"[74] The concept of public forums was established in 1939[75] and was expanded

---

73. Antonelli v. Hammond, 308 F. Supp. 1329 (S.Mass. 1970); Joyner v. Whiting, 477 F.2d 456 (4th Cir. 1973) (both fund cut-offs of college newspapers). See also "Adviser" sections of *Student Press Law Center Report* for lawsuits and out-of-court settlements by advisers. However, an adviser may be fired for refusing to censor when censorship was legally permissible. Jergeson v. Board of Trustees of School District No. 7, 476 P.2d 481 (1970).
74. Keyishian v. Board of Regents, 385 U.S. 589, 603 (1967).
75. Hague v. C.I.O., 307 U.S. 496 (1939).

over the next several decades to apply to open places such as streets, sidewalks and parks.[76] In these public forums, the state may regulate the time, place and manner of expression to preserve the primary purpose of the forum, but the restrictions must be "neutral" in that they are blind to the content of the expression. For example, a city could restrict all persons from shouting on the street after 10 p.m., but it could not restrict Marxists from shouting while permitting the Daughters of the American Revolution to harangue all night long. The state may place reasonable restrictions on the form of the speech but may not restrict the content.

According to this analysis, schools--as public forums--should be able to restrict only the time, place and manner of newspaper distribution. Also consistent with forum theory, schools could punish editors after distribution for libelous, obscene or otherwise unprotected speech (such as that which imminently incited violence). But the content of the speech should be considered only if it is libelous, obscene or inciteful. One cannot imagine a city prosecuting an adult who planned to distribute leaflets critical of the mayor, because police believed they would cause unrest.

The standard set in *Tinker* violated these tenets of forum theory. Justice Fortas' opinion indicated that speech could be banned--and the speaker punished--based on the content of the speech. What the substantial disruption test means is that if an idea, even one peacefully expressed, is so unorthodox that it provokes significant reaction from the listeners, then it may be censored and the speaker punished. This contradicts the essence of freedom of expression, which aims to protect unorthodoxy from the tyranny of the majority. Freedom of expression would be pallid indeed if it applied only to ideas that are generally accepted, ideas that do not jar the listener.

---

76. Schneider v. State, 308 U.S. 147 (1939); Cox v. New Hampshire, 312 U.S. 569 (1941); Jamison v. Texas, 318 U.S. 413 (1943); Martin v. Struthers, 319 U.S. 141 (1943); Saia v. New York City, 334 U.S. 558 (1948); Cox v. Louisiana [Cox I], 379 U.S. 536 (1965); Edwards v. South Carolina, 372 U.S. 229 (1963).

One might argue that restrictions on content of high school publications are necessary to prevent controversial articles from threatening the educational process, which is the primary purpose of schools. But the primary purpose of a forum may be protected only by time, place and manner restrictions--not by those of content. In all recent precedents, the Supreme Court has ruled that a hostile audience does not have a "heckler's veto" over a peaceful speaker. "It is firmly settled," the court wrote in 1969, "that under our Constitution the public expression of ideas may not be prohibited merely because the ideas are themselves offensive to some of their hearers."[77] If public high schools are to be treated consistently with other forums, schools should be permitted to impose time, place and manner restrictions only. They should not be able to regulate the content of the expression or punish a student for expressing unorthodox views.

One also might defend the court's position in *Tinker* on the grounds that schools are not public forums in the same sense as streets or parks. Laurence H. Tribe, for example, argues that:

Public facilities like schools and libraries, created not primarily for public interchange but for purposes closely linked to expression, have been treated as semi-public forums, with government enjoying power to preserve such tranquility as the facilities' central purpose requires--a power that would be denied in a true public forum--but not power to exclude peaceful speech or assembly compatible with that purpose.[78]

According to this argument, schools are not true public forums for two reasons: first, they historically have not been places to air political views, and second, they are institutions with a special purpose that is incompatible with the sound and fury associated with public forums. Proponents of this argument would say that the court in *Tinker* placed public schools in an intermediate category--"semi-public forums"--where

---

77. Street v. New York, 394 U.S. 576, 592 (1969). See also Edwards v. South Carolina, 372 U.S. 229 (1963); Gregory v. Chicago, 337 U.S. 11 (1969); Terminiello v. Chicago, 337 U.S. 1 (1949).
78. Laurence H. Tribe, *American Constitutional Law* (Mineola, N.Y.: Foundation Press, 1978), p. 690 (footnotes omitted).

rights may be exercised, but only consonant with the facilities' primary purpose.

It is true that not all public facilities are public forums. Places like public hospitals, libraries, golf courses, jails and military installations are known as "new" or "non-traditional" forums because there is normally little or no inherent right of expression in such places. But the Supreme Court has come in the last 20 years to treat schools not as "new" forums but as traditional public forums. In "new" forum cases, the court is concerned mostly with whether a restriction is applied evenhandedly, and asks only whether there is a reasonable relation between the rule and the state's responsibilities in the area.[79] But in school cases, the court has applied strict scrutiny and has adopted a much more activist posture in examining the merits of the restriction itself. This is true not just of student rights cases but also of decisions protecting the rights of teachers.[80] As the court noted, "The vigilant protection of constitutional freedoms is nowhere more vital than in the community of American schools."[81]

Unfortunately, the Supreme Court recently extended a *Tinker* -type test to a teacher case. In *Givhan v. Western Line Consolidated School District,* Justice Rehnquist, speaking for the court, said in a footnote: "When a teacher speaks publicly, it is generally the content of his statements that must be assessed to determine whether they 'in any way impeded the teacher's proper performance of his daily duties in the classroom or...interfered with the regular operation of the schools generally.'"[82] This extension is to be regretted, for it would permit a school to punish a

---

79. See, e.g. Brown v. Louisiana, 383 U.S. 131 (1966), a library case. The Supreme Court there indicated it would use a reasonable relation test for library rules that limited free speech of everyone equally.
80. Pickering v. Board of Education, 391 U.S. 563 (1968); City of Madison Joint School District v. Wisconsin Employment Relations Commission, 429 U.S. 167 (1976); Keyishian v. Board of Regents, 385 U.S. 589 (1967); Mt. Healthy v. Doyle, 429 U.S. 274 (1977); Shelton v. Tucker, 364 U.S. 479 (1960).
81. Shelton v. Tucker, 364 U.S. 479, 487 (1960).
82. 439 U.S 410 (1979) Emphasis and elipses in the original. The quotation within the footnote is from

teacher for expressing unpopular views, even if the expression was on his own time and even if he was not disruptive himself. Depending on how broadly the test was interpreted, it could permit a school to dismiss a Maxist teacher, if parents became very upset.

It is ironic that even in new forums the court has held that the government may not restrict expression based on content,[83] while in schools--which as public forums should have greater freedom of expression--the courts have condoned content-based restrictions. This again illustrates the paradox of *Tinker* and its progeny: While the courts generally treated schools as public forums and applied strict scrutiny, they abandoned--without acknowledging that they were doing any thing unusual--the most sacred principle of freedom of expression, that ideas shall not be censored on the basis of their content.[84] Schools should be treated like other public forums, so that content-based restrictions are impermissible. Because newspapers themselves are not disruptive--only the reaction to them--public forum theory should protect all expression in high school newspapers that is not obscene, libelous or an invasion of privacy.[85]

This probably also means that systems of prior restraint would be declared unconstitutional *per se*. The Supreme Court has expressed marked hostility to

---

Pickering v. Board of Education, 391 U.S. 563 (1968) at 572-73.

83. Adderly v. Florida, 385 U.S. 39 (1966); Brown v. Louisiana, 383 U.S. 131 (1966); Flower v. United States, 407 U.S. 197 (1972); Grayned v. City of Rockford, 408 U.S. 104 (1972); Greer v. Spock, 424 U.S. 828 (1976).

84. For a discussion of the types of forums, see Susan Garrison, 'Comment, The Public School as a Public Forum," *Texas Law Review*, Vol. 54, No. 1 (December 1975), pp. 90-125; Geoffrey R. Stone, "Fora Americana: Speech in Public Places," *The Supreme Court Review* 1974, pp. 233-280; Mark Tushnet, "Free Expression and the Young Adult: A Constitutional Framework," *University of Illinois Law Forum*, Vol. 1976, No. 3, pp. 746-62. My critique of the courts' application of forum theory to public schools draws from ideas in Tushnet.

85. Expression might also be subject to restrictions if it imminently incited violence or if it posed a significant risk to national security.

prior restraints,[86] so the acceptance of public high school newspapers as public forums, where constraints are evaluated under strict scrutiny, should mean that prior review is intolerable in high schools. Prior restraints are especially objectionable in high schools because administrators would be the censors, and the Supreme Court has ruled that administrative censorship is much less satisfactory than censorship by the courts as an independent branch of government.[87]

Eliminating prior restraints and content-based restrictions would solve the inadequacies that have marred *Tinker* and its progeny. These corrections would allow high school press law to blend into the pattern of Constitutional law, instead of sticking out like a tattered patch. Ending content-based restrictions would reduce the problem of vagueness and overbreadth in the substantial disruption test, allowing all points of view to blossom in the schools. Ending prior restraints would warm the spirits of high school editors who for so long have suffered under an ice age of chilling prior restraint. High school editors would gain rights coextensive with those of professional journalists, and in the process the newspapers themselves might become more professional. Securing legal rights for high school journalists would not immediately spawn a golden age of high school journalism. But it would be a good first step.

---

86. Near v. Minnesota, 283 U.S. 697 (1931); Bantam Books, Inc. v. Sullivan, 372 U.S. 58 (1963); New York Times Co. v. United States, 403 U.S. 713 (1971).
87. Freedman v. Maryland, 380 U.S. 51 (1965). See Leon Letwin, "Administrative Censorship of the Independent Student Press--Demise of the Double Standard?" *South Carolina Law Review*, Vol. 28, No. 5 (March 1977), pp. 565-85.

V

Socialization and Censorship

Whether or not censorship *should* exist, it is clear that it does exist. The survey for this book, as well as other studies, found widespread censorship in American public high schools. Many adolescents, therefore, grow up in an atmosphere of intolerance and authoritarianism, where order has priority over freedom. This finding raises important questions for the socialization of young people: Do students mimic the authoritarianism of their principals and journalism advisers, so that they grow up cherishing order over freedom? Do tight clamps on expression teach students to be suspicious of dissent and individual activism? If these questions are answered in the affirmative, schools with rigid censorship are inculcating into students values that are inimical to a democratic society, values that threaten a liberal political culture.

First, a caveat is necessary. No one would argue that the degree of censorship of a student newspaper alone determines the political attitudes of students for the rest of their lives. Censorship of a school newspaper is just one indication of a restrictive, intolerant educational atmosphere, and students are socialized not just in their classes but also at home and in the community. But, all this acknowledged, censorship still is very important because it sets a tone for the school. A school newspaper that truly serves as a public forum--where controversies are presented and points of view exchanged--will significantly contribute to an atmosphere in which vigorous debate of school and government problems is accepted and perhaps encouraged. Newspaper censorship also is important as an indicator of other constraints on expression in the school and community.

Because authoritarianism is a cultural attribute, rooted in society, it may be perpetuated in the traditional communities identified in Chapter II as bastions of censorship. Traditional communities usually are fairly closed, so young people are exposed primarily to the authoritarian values of their principals, teachers, parents and even peers. It is no wonder that students who now are censored are the most likely to approve of censorship. It is not surprising that where students and faculty alike are steeped in authoritarian traditions, court decisions have had so little impact on school censorship policies.

Authoritarian attitudes are subversive of democracy in almost every respect. Certainly a measure of conventionalism and obedience is important, but these should not stifle the tolerance that is essential in a democracy. Any liberal democracy requires a significant degree of tolerance from its citizens for two reasons: first, a citizen who is in the minority must be willing to accept the majority rule, and second, a citizen who is in the majority must be willing to respect the rights of minorities with whom he disagrees. The rigid value structures and contempt for differing ideas that characterize authoritarianism are inimical to a democratic system of government.

Several studies suggest that schools may be used to break up this cycle of authoritarianism in traditional communities. Gabriel A. Almond and Sidney Verba reported after their five-nation study that "education [is] the most important determinant of political attitudes" and that "interparty antagonism appears to be significantly reduced by education."[1] Another study, conducted by Robert D. Hess and Judith V. Torney, concluded that "the public school appears to be the most important and effective instrument of political socialization in the United States."[2]

---

1. Gabriel A. Almond and Sidney Verba, *The Civic Culture* (Boston: Little, Brown and Co., 1965), pp. 370-94. Some of the statements in *The Civic Culture* have been found flawed, but most of its broader conclusions and analysis still stand.
2. Robert D. Hess and Judith V. Torney, *The Development of Political Attitudes in Children* (Chicago; Aldine Publishing Co., 1967), p. 101.

Unfortunately, there are two difficulties with such generalizations. The first is that these studies normally show that people with much education have attitudes most compatible with democracy, not that the education itself is responsible for the improved socialization. It may be that people with more education have more democratic attitudes because they come from urban areas and upper middle class families. The second difficulty is that even if a causal relationship were demonstrated between education and political socialization, it would not be clear which level of education is most important to socialization, or whether a student newspaper could make a difference. It might be that high school is an unimportant period for an individual's political development.

A number of observers have glossed over these difficulties and have simply taken for granted that democratic treatment of high school students will ensure their democratic political development. In fact, the issue is far more complex than it at first appears, and the studies that exist do not necessarily support the assertion that adolescence is a crucial time for students to shape their political understandings. Indeed, until recently most studies have found that under normal circumstances little socialization occurs in high school. Robert D. Hess and David Easton reported on the basis of their research that, "while there was evidence of some change during the high school years, the magnitude of accumulated attitudes apparent in freshman classes indicated that the process of political socialization had been under way for some time and was nearing completion."[3]

Hess and Easton concluded that "the elementary-school years rather than high school years present the crucial time for...political socialization."[4] Other studies have found that a child's sense of political efficacy[5] and dissent toleration[6] have already largely crystallized by the time he enters high school.

---

3. Robert D. Hess and David Easton, "The Role of the Elementary School in Political Socialization," *The School Review*, Vol. 70, No. 3 (Autumn 1962), pp. 258-59.
4. *Ibid.*, p. 264.
5. David Easton and Jack Dennis, "The Child's Acquisition of Regime Norms: Political Efficacy," in Jack Dennis, ed., *Socialization to Politics* (New York: John Wiley & Sons, 1973), pp. 82-104.

A major study of the political socialization of adolescents by M. Kent Jennings and Richard G. Niemi found "strikingly little support" for the impact of the high school curriculum on socialization.[7] More relevant to student newspapers, the same researchers found little or no association between involvement in high school extra-curricular activities and political socialization. The authors tested for participation in student government, athletics, debate, music and clubs, but apparently did not test student journalism programs.[8]

These studies offer little support for the hypothesis that freedom of the press for high school newspapers-- and the degree of freedom in high schools generally-- affects the political attitudes of students. However, this may be a faulty interpretation because it relies on data that show only that curricula and activities *as they now are implemented* have little impact upon socialization. Further examination of the data suggests that civics classes and student activities are relatively unimportant only because they are redundant--they lead to skills and attitudes that students already have developed in elementary and junior high school. If high schools presented substantially new information or perspectives, socialization would advance through adolescence.

Support for this refined hypothesis comes in part from studies of socialization in high school of black students who have had less exposure in lower grades to democratic attitudes. Jennings and Niemi found a relationship between the number of civics classes taken by black students and their sense of political efficacy, where only a minimal relationship existed for whites (correlation is .05 for whites, .18 for Blacks). The blacks in the study came from disadvantaged homes more frequently than whites and were less politically aware, so Jennings and Niemi theorized that for blacks the civics curriculum was not redundant and did have an impact upon socialization. This is supported by

6. Jack Dennis, Leon Lindberg, Donald McCrone and Rodney Stiefbold, "Political Socialization to Democratic Orientations in Four Western Systems," in Dennis, ed., pp. 181-253.
7. M. Kent Jennings and Richard G. Niemi, *The Political Character of Adolescence* (Princeton, N.J.: Princeton Univ. Press, 1974), p. 190.
8. *Ibid.*, p. 230, n. 4.

statistics showing that the number of civics classes taken added to black students' political knowledge. The relationship between number of civics classes taken and sense of political efficacy was particularly strong among lower class blacks, which also indicates that the curriculum does have an impact on those who have not previously been exposed much to a democratic political culture.[9]

Jennings and Niemi also report a significantly higher correlation for blacks than for whites between number of courses taken and degree of civic tolerance (correlation for whites is .06, for blacks it is .22).[10] Unfortunately, Jennings and Niemi do not mention if a correlation exists for blacks between extra-curricular activities and political socialization. One may surmise that such a comparison would have been impossible because only 186 non-whites were surveyed,[11] and probably not enough of them were in extra-curricular activities to derive statistically significant correlations.

There is other evidence to support the refined hypothesis that exposure to new ideas in high school affects socialization. Some research has indicated that attitudes relating to competitive, allocative politics germinate only in late adolescence.[12] Joseph Adelson and his associates have found significant growth during high school years in understanding of, and support for, individual liberties.[13] Older youths tend to be more tolerant and less likely to adopt authoritarian solutions to political problems than are pre-high school age children.[14] Other researchers have found stepped-up divergence between opinions of students and

9. *Ibid.*, pp. 199-205.
10. *Ibid.*, p. 194.
11. *Ibid.*, p. 194.
12. David Easton and Jack Dennis, *Children in the Political System* (New York: McGraw Hill, 1969), see especially Chapters 4 and 12.
13. Judith Gallatin and Joseph Adelson, "Individual Rights and the Public Good," *Comparative Political Studies*, Vol. 13, No. 2 (July 1970), pp. 226-242.
14. Joseph Adelson and Robert P. O'Neil, "The Growth of Political Ideas in Adolescence: The Sense of Community," *Journal of Personality and Social Psychology*, Vol. 4, No. 3 (September 1966), pp. 295-306. See also Gail L. Zellman and David O. Sears, "Childhood Origins of Tolerance for

of their parents during adolescence,[15] and the students themselves report considerably increased interest in politics during their years in high school.[16] At the college level, a major study of students at Bennington College found that the students became significantly more liberal during their college years because they were exposed to liberal opinions and perspectives that they had not encountered before. A follow-up study found the increased liberalism among the Bennington students to have persisted 25 years later.[17] A different study found that Stanford University students who moved into a dormitory containing predominantly conservative students became more conservative over time.[18]

This research indicates that when people are exposed to new ideas--even if they are well beyond the elementary school level where most socialization now occurs--they will react to them and adjust their political attitudes and beliefs. Presumably one reason why little socialization takes place after elementary school is that the students usually remain in approximately similar circumstances and peer groups during high school and thereafter.

A recently reported study by Paul Allen Beck and M. Kent Jennings confirms the role that involvement in high school activities can play in socialization. They compared involvement level of high school seniors in 1965 in school activities (including student publications) with their participation in the political system eight years later. "School activities exert considerable influence on young adult participation," the researchers reported. "Their total effects exceed those of parent socio-economic status, parent civic orientations, and parent participation. Based on this evidence, the secondary role typically assigned to the schools in the political socialization process needs to

Dissent," *Journal of Social Issues,* Vol. 27, No. 2 (1971), pp. 109-136.
15. Robert E. Mainer, "Attitude Change in Intergroup Education Programs," in H.H. Remmers, ed., *Anti-Democratic Attitudes in American Schools* (Evanston, Ill.: Northwestern Univ. Press, 1963), p. 147.
16. Jennings and Niemi, p. 255.
17. Robert A. Baron and Donn Byrne, *Social Psychology* 2nd ed. (Boston: Allyn and Bacon, 1974), p. 264.
18. *Ibid.,* p. 264.

be reconsidered."[19] The authors add that, "High school activity does propel people into political activity later, even those who lack status and attitudinal advantages. In this respect, the school can serve as an alternative avenue for political mobilization."[20]

Cross-national surveys are useful in determining the influence of liberal and tolerant schools on democratic attitudes because such studies compare real differences in educational styles with real differences in political attitudes. While there is a danger of reading too much into the data and not accounting enough for historic national differences in education and attitudes, some studies indicate that relatively liberal educational systems help to inculcate democratic values into students. Almond and Verba found that participation in the classroom and the sense that one can protest a teacher's decision are positively associated with development of political attitudes important to a democratic society.[21] A different study of 4,500 adolescents in the United States and the Federal Republic of Germany found that:

> In both countries, school social climates which encourage independence of thought, emphasize concept (as opposed to rote) learning, minimize political ritual, and contain democratically run student peer groups, positively influence dissent toleration by stimulating better understanding of democratic principles and institutions.[22]

If the refined hypothesis is accepted, a new model of the influence of school newspapers on socialization may be proposed. This model states that newspapers have little or no impact when they are deferential, non-controversial and cover only school news. Such a newspaper offers nothing that is new to students. On the other hand, a vigorous, controversial school newspaper that comments on national and international affairs probably does enhance political socialization.

19. Paul Allen Beck and M. Kent Jennings, "Pathways to Participation," *The American Political Science Review,* Vol. 76, No. 1, (March 1982), p. 102.
20. *Ibid.,* pp. 105-106.
21. Almond and Verba, pp. 287-294.
22. H. Dean Nielsen, *Tolerating Political Dissent* (Stockholm, Sweden: Almqvist & Wiksell International, 1977), p. 11.

This newspaper will present political issues before the students, and if the presentations are controversial they may excite some interest in the issues. As Jennings and Niemi found, adolescence is a period when people become dramatically more interested in politics and the larger world.[23]

A controversial school newspaper that criticizes school policies also will acquaint students with the concepts of democratic debate and decision making. It may help to wean them from the obsessive fear of conflict that often pervades traditional communities. While students have been exposed to criticisms of congressmen and the president in the commercial press, such debates over national issues and national figures tend to be far removed from the world of the high school student. Particularly in a traditional community where rigid consensus is a dominant value, a student will not necessarily learn from the daily newspaper or television news that debate is healthy not just at the national level but also at the local level. A school newspaper, published by students, may help young people realize that dissent and debate are acceptable--even worthwhile--in a democracy. Robust debates on news and editorial pages expose them to a variety of political views and build their tolerance. If the newspaper serves as an outlet where students can air their complaints and frustrations about school policies, the newspaper might inculcate in the students the sense that they can complain when they believe they have been treated unjustly. In short, the newspaper might enhance the students' sense of political efficacy and competence, as well as increase their interest in politics and tolerance of other views.

Of course, vigorous school newspapers will not by themselves revolutionize student attitudes. Students are socialized not just in schools but also in families and communities. Some of these agents of socialization might teach values that conflict with those engendered by the school newspaper, but at least the newspaper would expose students to democratic values and attitudes. A newspaper, especially one that is published frequently, is a democratic force in students' lives, showing them that there are alternatives to the authoritarian outlook. In traditional communities where authoritarian values go unquestioned, a vigorous student newspaper would make

---

23. Jennings and Niemi, p. 255.

democratic inroads by serving as perhaps the only agent for democratic socialization. The newspaper would be a voice in the wilderness, but a voice nonetheless.

VI

CONCLUSION

More than 120 years have passed since Peter Lander was thrashed in class for calling his schoolmaster "Old Jack Seaver" one day after school. The world has progressed in many ways since 1859, but Lander would sill recognize the authoritarianism that lingers in the schools of many traditional communities. Despite revolutionary changes in living standards and technology during the last century, high school students live in a twilight zone in which their rights are ignored and their opinions are scorned. High school students are among the last people whom it is still respectable to treat as second-class citizens--people who have no "rights" but only such tidbits of freedom as the school administration deigns to provide. This study has examined the issues of student press rights from four perspectives--empirical analysis, social policy, the law and socialization--and all of these perspectives point in the same direction: that high school students should have the same rights of freedom of the press as exist in adult society.

These perspectives also point to censorship in most high schools that is oppressive and stultifying. More than 80 percent of schools surveyed for this study report some censorship or potential for censorship, and at many schools the pressure is constant and unrelenting. With the surveys came countless horror stories: of the Indiana editor who was suspended for three days because she reported (correctly) that her school was making a profit from the federally funded school lunch program; of the Iowa principal who censored articles about the school's failure to comply with laws mandating equal access for the handicapped; of the students who were threatened with poor grades or college recommendations because they protested censorship; of the students who were informed that their adviser would be fired if they demanded freedom of the press. The list goes on and on.

One wonders what goes through the minds of students who know that they are being censored illegally. The survey for this book showed that more than 90 percent of student editors realize that they have a legal right to print editorials attacking school policies, yet most of those same editors reported censorship. How disillusioning to learn that your school--the body of government with which you deal the most--has no qualms about breaking the law! Cynicism is the byproduct when students are taught in civics class to obey the law but learn in journalism class that school officials feel no compunctions about violating the Constitution.

Even more disturbing is that at many schools the students are so cowed or restrained that they never write anything worth censoring. Sometimes this is because of intimidation or pressure from the newspaper adviser or principal. Often it is voluntary--a reflection of the students' honest belief that "kids" should not criticize school officials. This indicates an abdication of the citizen's responsibility to participate in a democracy, as well as an extreme and unhealthy fear of conflict. In essence the school becomes what Almond and Verba call a subject political culture--one in which the citizen is merely a passive observer of all that the government does.[1] Although the student's formal education in civics classes stresses democratic participation in government, in practice the student is imbued with authoritarian values that stress obedience to every whim of the principal. This may explain why so many people--adults as well as children--say in the abstract that they support freedom of speech but then add that speech-making communists should be jailed.[2]

1. Gabriel A. Almond and Sydney Verba, *The Civic Culture* (Boston: Little, Brown and Co., 1965), pp. 24-26.
2. See Gail L. Zellman and David O. Sears, "Childhood Origins of Tolerance for Dissent," *Journal of Social Issues* Vol. 27, No. 2 (1971), pp. 109-136. See also Richard M. Merelman, "Democratic Politics and the Culture of American Education," *The American Political Science Review*, Vol. 74, No. 2 (June 1980), p. 319.

Students accept this subject culture because it often is all they know. Small traditional communities are incestuous, and when anybody in the "family" steps out of line everyone else knows about it instantly and displays stern disapproval. Students steeped in this climate do not question it, and when they sit down in journalism class, they aim to please. As Erich Fromm has argued, some people may be willing to sacrifice the confusion and conflict of democratic participation for the order and stability of autocracy. To some extent Fromm's thesis is applicable to traditional communities, for the students readily accept constraints so that they will avoid the unpleasantness, confusion and divisiveness that would accompany the exercise of their rights. The students, in other words, learn to escape from freedom. As one student commented on a questionnaire, "getting along is what it's all about"[3]

Not only do such attitudes undermine democratic political socialization, but they also make it very difficult for other students to break the ice and demand their rights. An over-assertive student runs the risk of ostracism for his non-conformism. He becomes a 20th century Hester Prynne, with his own scarlet letter "A"--for Activist. When Charles Reineke, editor of a school newspaper in Cobb County, Georgia, sued his school administration in the fall of 1979 for repeated censorship, his classmates telephoned death threats, called him a "dirty commie" and urged him to "go to Iran." The principal reportedly announced over the public address system, "I know this is illegal, but I would like each of you to pray for us as we go to court today." When the federal district judge ruled in favor of Reineke, a crowd of about 60 students, led by the student body president, burned copies of the newspaper to show their contempt for the newspaper staff.[4] Charles Reineke was willing to become a pariah for the sake of freedom of the press, but he was an exception. Most editors, even if they chafe at censorship, are willing to "go along to get along."

Court decisions have had little impact on censorship policies in traditional communities precisely because

3. See Erich Fromm, *Escape From Freedom* (New York: Rinehart & Co., 1941).
4. "High School Editor Sues...Wins Landmark Case," *Student Press Law Center Report*, Vol. III, No.2 (Spring 1980), pp. 2-3.

authoritarian, conformist attitudes are so deep-seated. The students themselves often do not see themselves as victims, and if they do, they may be willing to let it slide rather than raise a fuss. The law should not be seen as a magic wand that will rid schools of censorship with a swish through the air, but as a useful tool if the students have the fortitude to use it. The law is important because it endows the students' cause with legitimacy and provides a tool of last resort. However, ultimately censorship will be eradicated only when attitudes change--attitudes of principals, teachers, parents and students themselves. As Judge Learned Hand once observed:

> I often wonder whether we do not rest our hopes too much upon constitutions, upon laws and upon courts. These are false hopes; believe me, these are false hopes. Liberty lies in the hearts of men and women; when it dies there, no constitution, no law, no court can save it; no constitution, no law, no court can even do much to help it. While it lies there it needs no constitution, no law, no court to save it.[5]

The great irony is that the schools that most need the fresh air and democratic voices are those that are least likely to get them. Vigorous school newspapers are precisely what traditional communities need, because the newspapers would provide an alternative to the authoritarianism that dominates the local culture. But precisely because such a newspaper is an alternative--because it conflicts with accepted values--it is unlikely to sprout in a traditional community. Censorship and community hostility would choke it in its infancy. So the catch-22 is that an activist school newspaper requires a supportive culture of democratic attitudes, but democratic attitudes require some source such as a vigorous school newspaper. If a school has neither democratic attitudes nor a vigorous school newspaper, it is unlikely to sprout either.

If the legal system cannot ensure freedom of the press for high school students, and if attitudes in traditional communities are slow to admit freedom, is

---

5. "Spirit of Liberty," a speech in New York City, May 21, 1944. Irving Dilliard, ed., *The Spirit of Liberty: Papers and Addresses of Learned Hand* (New York: Alfred A. Knopf, 1952), pp. 189-90.

there any hope that First Amendment rights of students will be realized in traditional communities? There is hope and there will be change, but it will be a painstaking metamorphosis from traditional to liberal values. The law will help, for it raises expectations of students, and when they are willing to accept derision and ostracism the law may be invoked to protect their rights. Attorneys for school districts may also invoke the law in preparing tolerant publication policies and in advising their clients that censorship is impermissible. Slowly, too, the ranks of principals and journalism advisers will be joined by former activist high school journalists, adults who remember that as youths they chafed at the bit of paternalism. Finally, the traditional bases of conservative school districts will erode, as mobility increases and people with new values and expectations move into conservative communities. Change will come, but slowly.

The practical differences between a vigorous school newspaper and a passive one are best illustrated with examples. About a dozen editors included copies of their newspapers with their surveys, and a comparison of the papers at two schools shows how different the newspapers can be:

--A North Carolina high school newspaper had three articles on its front page: a lead article about the new principal, an account of a meeting of the Future Business Leaders of America club, and a two-paragraph blurb about college representatives coming to the school. The article about the principal began by quoting him as saying that he subscribed to the Biblical quote: "train up a child in the way he should go; and when he is old, he will not depart from it" (Proverbs 22:6). The article ended: "In the first pep rally of this school year, Mr. _____ said we have the best high school in North Carolina. We agree that _____ is a great school and one that is under equally great leadership. Best of luck in the future Mr. _____." The editorial page contained an inspirational "Message from the Principal," a record review, a list of the staff, and the lengthy publications policy.

--In contrast, a Texas newspaper contained articles about "white flight" from the school district, an article and an editorial about sex education and a four-page section on "Election '80," including in-depth analyses of each presidential candidate's positions on various issues. The newspaper also contained extensive coverage of the nominees for homecoming queen and other articles of strictly school interest. Other issues of this newspaper contained a special four-page section on teenage sexuality, thoughtful editorials about a range of school, community and national issues, and several articles and commentaries about an assistant principal who had resigned under pressure after divulging that he was a homosexual. The newspaper is not particularly liberal--it editorialized in favor of draft registration--but it impresses the reader with its thorough and provocative treatment of a range of issues.

The differences are stark. The former newspaper is essentially a public relations newsletter for the administration, neither thought provoking nor interesting to read. The latter newspaper is clearly independent of the administration and goes beneath the surface with its articles and editorials. The second newspaper is both an outlet for students and a positive socializing influence upon them. It fills in the school setting the role that a good commercial newspaper fills in a city. It also is an exception.

Most high school newspapers purvey only pabulum, so that is all the students learn to digest. The students shy away from conflict and controversy and learn to be subjects rather than citizens. Those editors who dare to be different are punished or ostracized, tarnishing their respect for the First Amendment. The remedy is to provide students with the same rights of freedom of the press that the professional media enjoy, releasing them from the twilight zone of paternalism. The courts alone cannot accomplish such changes, but they can help. True freedom of the press for high school students must be rooted in a firmer base of democratic attitudes in each community. This will come with time, for the bastions of order and authoritarianism--traditional communities --eventually will crumble and be replaced by more open and fluid communities. When this happens, the content of school newspapers will be spicier, at times unpalatable to some people. Such is the price a democratic society pays for permitting free expression. It is a price worth paying to wean high school students of their diet of pabulum.

Appendix

[This is the questionnaire that was sent to 500 high schools as part of the research for this study. The proportions that chose each response do not always add up to 100 percent because sometimes respondents did not answer all the questions. The questionnaire that was sent out was six pages long, printed on both sides of three sheets of paper.]

*   *   *

Nicholas D. Kristof
E-31 Lowell House
Harvard University
Cambridge, MA 02138
(617) 498-2932

SURVEY

(This survey form should be given to the student newspaper editor. If your school does not have a student newspaper or if for some other reason the questions are not applicable, please return the survey with an explanatory note. A stamped return envelope is provided. Because of the need to preserve a random sample, I will contact you again if the survey is not returned. Thank you for your co-operation.)

To: student newspaper editors

From: Nicholas D. Kristof, senior in Government Department at Harvard College

This is a very important survey distributed to 500 public high schools around the United States. Your school was selected at random to participate, and I hope you will answer the questions and mail the form back to me as soon as possible. A stamped return envelope is enclosed. The purpose of the survey is to determine the amount of editorial freedom high school newspapers have today. The results will be incorporated into a senior honors thesis at Harvard College.

Your responses will be kept confidential and you may remain anonymous if you wish. Of course, the survey will be useful only if the questionnaires are answered honestly. Please think about the questions--think about what you really would do in the circumstances described--and answer all the questions honestly and to the best of your ability. Please feel free to discuss your feelings or experience more fully at the end of the questionnaire or on a separate sheet. However, please return the survey form as soon as possible.

1. Has there been any censorship of a student publication at your school in the last three years? (Please circle your answer.)

   47.5%   a) no censorship

   33.1%   b) one or two incidents of censorship in three years

   12.6%   c) three to ten incidents of censorship in three years

   5.8%   d) there has been repeated and continual censorship

2. If you reported that there has been censorship in your school, was the censorship in (circle as many as apply):

   81.5%   a) the student newspaper

   0.7%   b) the student yearbook

   2.7%   c) an unofficial or "underground" newspaper

   9.7%   d) other (literary magazines)

   0.6%   a and b

   2.1%   a and c

   1.4%   a and d

3. Does the newspaper adviser or school administration discourage the newspaper from probing in controversial areas?

   32.4% a) yes

   66.5% b) no

4. How restricted is your newspaper in covering sensitive subjects?

   18.0% a) Completely unrestricted. I can't imagine any censorship here.

   76.3% b) Somewhat restricted. The school might not let us cover some subjects but for the most part we are allowed to write what we want.

    4.7% c) Very restricted. The administration lets us print only what it likes to see.

5. Suppose the newspaper staff wanted to print the following in an editorial: "Far too much money at this school goes for athletics and not nearly enough to academics. The school administration has the wrong priorities, and until things get straightened out a diploma from here will not mean much." Do you think you would be permitted to write that in your school paper?

   56.1% a) yes

   18.7% b) no

   24.5% c) not sure

6. Do you believe you have a legal right to print the above statement?

   91.7% a) yes

    1.1% b) no

    7.2% c) not sure

7. Does the administration at your school think you have any legal rights of freedom of the press?

   64.4% a) yes

    6.8% b) no

   28.8% c) not sure

8. Are you familiar with the legal rights of high school journalists?

   22.3% a) no

   62.6% b) somewhat familiar

   14.4% c) very familiar

9. Suppose you heard that a half-dozen parents were circulating a petition demanding that the principal be fired. Would you:

   35.3% a) wait and see what happens

   29.5% b) assign a reporter and ask him or her to write a small article

   34.2% c) assign one or more reporters and ask them to write a major article

10. Regardless of your answer above, suppose you decided to include a major article on the front page about the petition drive and criticisms of the principal. Do you think the administration would let you do this?

   36.3% a) yes

   32.4% b) no

   30.6% c) not sure

11. Would you be worried that if you tried to run such an article about the principal it might be censored or the administration might try to punish you or the newspaper?

   58.6% a) yes

   39.6% b) no

12. Suppose a group of students known as the "smokers" (because they smoked cigarettes near the school during the lunch hour) threatened to boycott classes because of harassment by school staff. What would you do?

   22.3% a) probably nothing for now

   43.9% b) write a short article

   32.0% c) write a long article

13. How would you describe your newspaper?

28.4%　a)　Not controversial. Covers positive school news and does not criticize teachers or school officials.

68.0%　b)　Sometimes controversial. Includes some news or editorials critical of school staff.

2.5%　c)　Often controversial. Includes news or editorials strongly critical of school staff and makes little effort to be "polite."

14. If you responded a or b above, why is the newspaper not more controversial? (Circle as many as apply.)

23.6%　a)　I don't think a school newspaper should spend much time criticizing the school or people who work in it.

13.3%　b)　We're not allowed to be more controversial.

50.9%　c)　Other [The two most common types of responses were, first, that the school had little that was controversial to cover, and second, that school newspapers should be positive and should not stress controversy too much.]

3.3%　a and b

3.3%　a and c

1.5%　b and c

0.7%　a, b and c

15. What rights do you think you should have?

54.0%　a)　same rights as adult newspaper reporters and editors

42.8%　b)　some rights, but under supervision of the school administration

1.8%　c)　the administration should have final authority over the newspaper

16. If a conflict arose at your school between the administration and the newspaper staff, whose side do you think the adviser would take?

10.8%   a)   administration's

45.3%   b)   students'

14.7%   c)   would not take sides

28.4%   d)   not sure

17. Does your school have a written policy governing what may be printed in student publications?

14.4%   a)   yes

80.9%   b)   no

18. Suppose an article you write this year is censored. What would you do?

28.4%   a)   nothing

58.6%   b)   complain and perhaps circulate petitions

7.9%   c)   take the case to court

19. Who has the final right of approval of articles and advertisements in your school's newspaper?

14.0%   a)   students

18.3%   b)   administration

62.2%   c)   adviser

20. Who assigns articles? (Circle as many as apply.)

9.7%   a)   the adviser

46.8%   b)   student editor(s)

3.6%   c)   other

37.1%   a and b

1.4%   other combinations

21. Who edits articles? (Circle as many as apply.)

12.9%   a)   the adviser

19.4%   b)   student editor(s)

0.7%   c)   other

61.5%   a and b

1.4%   b and c

3.2%   a, b and c

22. How is the editor of your newspaper selected?

    56.8%   a)   appointed by newspaper adviser

    16.2   b)   elected by newspaper staff

     7.6   c)   chosen by outgoing editor(s)

     2.2   d)   other

     3.2   a and b

    10.8   a and c

     1.1   other combinations

23. About how many students go to your high school? (If there are more than four years in the school, how many students are in the top four grades?) [Mean was 1,011 with a standard deviation of 778; median was 950; range was 30 to 6,000.]

24. What grades are in the school?

    26.3%   a)   10th through 12th grade

    60.1%   b)   9th through 12th grade

    12.2%   c)   other [most frequently 7th through 12th grades and 1st through 12th grades]

25. Is your high school in:

    10.1%   a)   a large city (population of more than 150,000)

    65.1%   b)   a small city or suburbs

    23.7%   c)   the country

26. How would you describe the area in which your school is located and from which the students come?

    13.7%   a)   upper middle class

    55.0%   b)   middle class

    27.3%   c)   working class

27. How often does your newspaper come out?

    17.6%   a)   every two weeks

     6.5%   b)   weekly

    52.9%   c)   monthly

22.3%   d)   other [either every three weeks or once
              or twice per term]

28. Is your newspaper

    69.8%   a)   printed commercially
    29.5%   b)   duplicated within the school

29. Does your newspaper receive funds from the school?

    50.4%   a)   yes
    48.9%   b)   no

Please use the remaining space to discuss any
incidents of censorship at your school or any concerns
you have. Thank you for your help.

(Optional) your name _____ title ____

Regional breakdown of surveys returned:

    West   19.8%
    Central   34.2%
    South   22.3%
    East   23.0%

Bibliography

Articles

Adelson, Joseph and Robert P. O'Neil. "The Growth of Political Ideas in Adolescence: The Sense of Community." *Journal of Personality and Social Psychology*. Vol. 4, No. 3 (September 1966), pp. 295-306.

Anrig, Gregory R. "Those High School Protestors: Can Boards Put Up With Much More?" *American School Board Journal*. Vol. 157, No. 4 (October 1969), pp. 20-24.

Banta, Robert Edward. "Note, Constitutional Law--First Amendment--School Authorities May Prohibit High School Students' Distribution of Sex Questionnaires to prevent Possible Psychological Harm to Other Students." *Vanderbilt Law Review*. Vol. 31, No. 1 (January 1978), pp. 173-182.

Beck, Paul Allen and M. Kent Jennings. "Pathways to Participation." *The American Political Science Review*. Vol. 76, No. 1 (March 1982), p. 94.

"Behind the Schoolhouse Gate: Sex and the Student Pollster." *New York University Law Review*. Vol. 54, No. 1 (April 1979), pp. 161-203.

Berkman, Richard L. "Students in Court: Free Speech and Functions of Schooling in America." *Harvard Educational Review*. Vol. 40, No. 4 (November 1970), pp. 567-595.

"Board Gives in to Suit; No Review, Meetings Open." *Student Press Law Center Report*. Vol. II, No. 3 (fall 1979), p. 14.

Bowen, John. "'Captive Voices' Brings New Study." *Communication: Journalism Education Today*. Vol. 9 (spring 1976), pp. 18-22.

Boyer, John H. "Court Upholds Newspaper Suppression." *Scholastic Editor*. Vol. 59, No. 4 (April/May 1980), pp. 29-32.

Broussard, E. Joseph and C. Robert Blackmon. "Advisers, Editors and Principals Judge First Amendment Cases." Journalism Quarterly. Vol. 55, No. 4 (winter 1978), pp. 797-799.

Broussard, E. Joseph and C. Robert Blackmon. "Principals Think They Can Do What Congress Cannot--Abridge Freedom of the High School Press." *Quill and Scroll*. October/November 1980, pp. 15-17.

Brown, Donal. "Everything You've Always Wanted to Know About Doing a Sex Survey." *Scholastic Editor*. Vol. 58, No. 2 (October/November 1978), pp. 29-31.

Carmody, Dierdre. "School Paper's Article on Drug Dealer Spurs Battle on Press Rights." *The New York Times,* March 26, 1981, p. 1.

Clark, Todd, ed. "Special Issue: The Question of Academic Freedom." *Social Education*. Vol. 39, No. 4 (April 1975).

Claypool, Forrest E. "Note, Public Forum Theory In the Educational Setting: The First Amendment and the Student Press." *University of Illinois Law Forum*. Vol. 1979, No. 4, pp. 879-913.

Cox, Benjamin C. "The Varieties of Censorial Experience: Toward a Definition of Censorship." *The High School Journal*. Vol. 62, No. 8 (May 1979), pp. 311-319.

De Witt, Karen. "School Press, With More Articles on Controversial Topics, Is Under Increasing Attack." *The New York Times*. Vol. CXXVIII, No. 44, 209 (May 6, 1979), Section 1, p. 26.

Diamond, Priscilla. "Interference With the Rights of Others: Authority to Restrict Students' First Amendment Rights." *Journal of Law and Education*. Vol. 8, No. 3(July 1979), pp. 347-358.

Eagles, William A. "Note, Constitutional Law--Right of

Public School Children to Receive Information--
*Minarcini v. Stringsville City School District."
WakeForest Law Review.* Vol. 13, No. 4 (winter 1977),
pp. 834-841.

Feldman, Sam. "To Publish Underground Newspapers."
Communication: Journalism Education Today. Vol. 23,
No. 1 (fall 1968), p. 7.

"The First Amendment Gets No Respect." *Student Press
Law Center Report.* Vol. III, No. 2 (Spring 1980),
p. 43.

Fischer, Louis and Gail Paulus Sorenson. "Censorship,
Schooling and the Law." *The High School Journal.*
Vol. 62, No. 8 (May 1979), pp. 320-326.

Freeman, M.D.A. "The Rights of Children in the
International Year of the Child." Lord Lloyd of
Hampstead, ed., *Current Legal Problems 1980.* London:
Stevens & Sons, 1980.

Fuller, Lawrence B. "Students' Rights of Expression:
The Decade since *Tinker." The English Journal.* Vol.
68, No. 9 (December 1979), p. 11.

Gallatin, Judith and Joseph Adelson. "Individual Rights
and the Public Good." *Comparative Political Studies.*
Vol. 3, No. 2 (July 1970), pp. 226-242.

Garrison, Susan. "Comment, The Public School as a
Public Forum." *Texas Law Review.* Vol. 54, No. 1
(December 1975), pp. 90-125.

Garvey, John H. "Children and the First Amendment."
Texas Law Review. Vol. 57, No. 3 (February 1979),
pp. 321-379.

Gold, Barbara. "The Student Press--An Update."
Inequality in Education. No. 20 (July 1975), pp.
74-79.

Gutmann, Amy. "Children, Paternalism and Education: A
Liberal Argument." *Philosophy & Public Affairs.* Vol.
9, No. 4 (Summer 1980), pp. 338-358.

Hansen, Kent A. "Obscenity, Profanity and the High
School Press." *Willamette Law Review.* Vol. 15 (summer
1979), pp. 507-529.

Hentoff, Nat. "Making the First Amendment as Real as

Sex." *The Civil Liberties Review*. Vol. 4, No. 6 (March/April 1978), pp. 51-54.

Hess, Robert D. and David Easton. "The Role of the Elementary School in Political Socialization." *The School Review*. Vol. 70, No. 3 (Autumn 1962), pp. 257-265.

"High School Editor Sues...Wins Landmark Case." *Student Press Law Center Report*. Vol. III, No. 2 (Spring 1980), pp. 2-3.

Horine, Don D. "How Principals, Advisers and Editors View the High School Newspaper." *Journalism Quarterly*. Vol. XLIII (Summer 1966), pp. 339-345.

James, Max H. "Propaganda or Education? Censorship and School Journalism." *Arizona English Bulletin*. Vol. 13, No. 1 (October 1970), pp. 37-41. EDRS Document ED 045675.

Janson, Donald. "Jury Decides Not to Query Adviser to School's Paper." *The New York Times,* April 1, 1981, p. B2.

Janson, Donald. "School Paper's Adviser Facing Court Order." *The New York Times,* March 27, 1981, p. B1.

"Judge Upholds Newspaper Seizure." *Student Press Law Center Report*. Vol. II, No. 1 (Winter 1978-79), p. 25.

Jennings, M. Kent. "Comment on Richard Merelman's 'Democratic Politics and the Culture of American Education.'" *The American Political Science Review*. Vol. 74, No. 2 (June 1980), p. 333.

Koch John B. "Constitutional Law--The Children's Crusade for Constitutional Recognition." *West Virginia Law Review*. Vol. 78, No. 2 (February 1976), pp. 192-212.

Kohler, Mary. "The Rights of Children--An Unexplored Constituency." *Social Policy*. Vol. 1, No. 6 (March/April 1971), pp. 36-43.

Krafte, Jill H. *"Tinker's* Legacy: Freedom of the Press in Public High Schools." *DePaul Law Review*. Vol. 28 (Winter 1979), pp. 387-428.

Ladd, Edward T. "Civil Liberties for Students--At What

Age?" *Journal of Law and Education.* Vol. 3, No. 2 (April 1974), pp. 251-266.

Letwin, Leon. "Administrative Censorship of the Independent Student Press--Demise of the Double Standard?" *South Carolina Law Review.* Vol. 28, No. 5 (March 1977), pp. 565-585.

Mann, Robert B. "Prior Restraints in Public High Schools." *Yale Law Journal.* Vol. 82, No. 6 (May 1973), pp. 1325-1336.

Merelman, Richard M. "Democratic Politics and the Culture of American Education.'" *The American Political Science Review.* Vol. 74, No. 2 (June 1980), p. 319.

Nolte, M. Chester. "The Student Press and the Ways You Can Control It." *American School Board Journal.* Vol. 165, No. 3 (March 1978), pp. 35-36.

"Note, First Amendment--Prior Restraint--Board of Education Rule Requiring Prior Submission of Private Student Newspapers is Unconstitutionally Vague and Overbroad-- *Nitzberg v. Parks.* " *Maryland Law Review* Vol. 35, No. 3 (1976), pp. 512-522.

Nyka, James J. "Censorship of Illinois High School Papers." *Communication: Journalism Education Today.* Vol. 12, No. 4 (summer 1979), pp. 6-9.

"Opinion Roundup." *Public Opinion.* Vol. 2, No. 4 (August/September 1979), pp. 36-40.

"'Press' Four-Letter Word in Illinois." *Student Press Law Center Report.* Spring 1978, p. 9.

Pressman, Robert. "Students' Right to Write and Distribute." *Inequality in Education.* No. 15 (November 1973), pp. 63-83.

Rasmussen, Pat. "The Mullen Decision Conflicts With Journalists' First Amendment Rights." *Quill and Scroll.* October/November 1980, pp. 18-19.

Redden, James A. "Opinion of the Attorney General, No. 7630." June 5, 1978. Salem, Ore.: Office of the Attorney General.

Redden, James A. "Opinion of the Attorney General, No. 7735." March 16, 1979. Salem, Ore.: Office of the

Attorney General.

Sewell, Michael. "Journalism, Political Science Classes Agree, Disagree on First Amendment Questions." *Journalism Educator*. Vol. 35, No. 3 (October 1980), pp. 8-10.

Simpson, Michael D. Letter to Oregon Attorney General James A. Redden, re: First Amendment rights of high school journalists. April 5, 1979, 5 pp. Unpublished.

Stone, Geoffrey R. "Fora Americana: Speech in Public Places." *The Supreme Court Review 1974*, pp. 233-280.

Tushnet, Mark. "Free Expression and the Young Adult: A Constitutional Framework." *University of Illinois Law Forum*. Vol. 1976, No. 3, pp. 746-762.

Weiner, Lois. "Captive Voices: Are They Still?" *Communication: Journalism Education Today*. Vol. 12, No. 3 (spring 1979), pp. 4-7.

Zellman, Gail L. and David O. Sears. "Childhood Origins of Tolerance for Dissent." *Journal of Social Issues*. Vol. 27, No. 2 (1971), pp. 109-136.

Zirkel, Perry A. "A Test on Supreme Court Decisions Affecting Education." *Phi Delta Kappan*. Vol. 59, No. 8 (April 1978), pp. 521-522.

Books

Adorno, T, E. Frenkel-Brunswick, D. Levinson and N. Sanford. *The Authoritarian Personality*. New York: Harper, 1950.

Almond, Gabriel A. and Sidney Verba. *The Civic Culture*. Boston: Little, Brown and Co., 1965.

Aries, Philippe. *Centuries of Childhood*. Robert Baldick, trans. New York: Alfred A. Knopf, 1962.

Barron, Jerome A. *Freedom of the Press for Whom?* Bloomington, Ind.: Indiana Univ. Press, 1973.

Birmingham, John, ed. *Our Time is Now: Notes From the High School Underground*. New York: Praeger Publishers 1970.

Bolmeier, Ed C. *Legal Limits of Authority Over the*

Pupil. Charlottesville, Va.: Michie Company, 1970.

Brown, Roger. *Social Psychology*. New York: Free Press, 1965.

Christie, Richard and Marie Jahoda. *Studies in the Scope and Method of "The Authoritarian Personality."* Glencoe, Ill.: Free Press, 1954.

Cohen, William and John Kaplan. *Bill of Rights*. Mineola, N.Y.: Foundation Press, 1976.

Davis, James E., ed. *Dealing With Censorship*. Urbana, Ill.: National Council of Teachers of English, 1979.

Dennis, Jack, ed. *Socialization to Politics: A Reader*. New York: John Wiley & Sons, 1973.

Denzin, Norman K. *Childhood Socialization*. San Francisco: Jossey-Bass Publishers, 1977.

Dewey, John. *Democracy and Education*. New York: Macmillan Co. 1924.

Dworkin, Ronald. *Taking Rights Seriously*. Cambridge, Mass.: Harvard Univ. Press, 1978.

Easton, David and Jack Dennis. *Children in the Political System*. New York: McGraw Hill, 1969.

Fager, Christopher B. *Ownership and Control of the Student Press: A First Amendment Analysis*. Washington, D.C.: Student Press Law Center, mimeo.

Flygare, Thomas J. *The Legal Rights of Students*. Bloomington, Ind.: Phi Delta Kappa Educational Foundation, 1975.

Friedenberg, Edgar Z. *Coming of Age in America*. New York: Random House, 1965.

Fromm, Erich. *Escape from Freedom*. New York: Rinehart & Co., 1941.

Gaddy, Dale. *Rights and Freedoms of Public School Students: Directions From the 1960's*. Topeka, Kan.: National Organization on Legal Problems in Education, 1971.

Gee, E. Gordon and David J. Sperry. *Education Law and the Public Schools: A Compendium*. Boston: Allyn and

Bacon, 1978.

Glock, Charles Y., ed. *Survey Research in the Social Sciences*. New York: Russell Sage Foundation, 1967.

Gordon, C. Wayne. *The Social System of the High School*. Glencoe, Ill.: Free Press, 1957.

Greenberg, Edward S. *Political Socialization*. New York: Atherton Press, 1970.

Greenstein, Fred I. *Children and Politics*. New Haven, Conn.: Yale Univ. Press, 1965.

Gunther, Gerald. *Cases and Materials on Constitutional Law*. Mineola, N.Y.: Foundation Press, 1975.

Gunther, Gerald. *1979 Supplement to Cases and Materials on Constitutional Law, 9th ed., and Cases and Materials on Individual Rights in Constitutional Law*, 2nd ed. Mineola, N.Y.: Foundation Press, 1979

Hentoff, Nat. *The First Freedom*. New York: Delacorte Press, 1980.

Hess, Robert D. and Judith V. Torney. *The Development of Political Attitudes in Children*. Chicago: Aldine Publishing, 1967.

Hyman, Herbert H. *Political Socialization*. New York: Free Press, 1959.

Hyman, Herbert H. *Survey Design and Analysis*. Glencoe, Ill.: Free Press, 1955.

Jennings, M. Kent and Richard G. Niemi. *The Political Character of Adolescence*. Princeton, N.J.: Princeton Univ. Press, 1974.

Johnston, Edgar G. and Roland C. Faunce. *Student Activities In Secondary Schools*. New York: Ronald Press, 1952.

Kemerer, Frank R. and Kenneth L. Deutsch. *Constitutional Rights and Student Life*. St. Paul, Minn.: West Publishing, 1979.

Kilzer, Louis R., Harold H. Stephenson and H. Orville Nordberg. *Allied Activities in the Secondary School*. New York: Harper & Bros., 1956.

Kirscht, John P. and Ronald C. Dillehay. *Dimensions of Authoritarianism: A Review of Research and Theory*. Lexington, Ky.: Univ. of Kentucky Press, 1967.

Knight, Richard S. *Students' Rights: Issues in Constitutional Freedoms*. Boston: Houghton Mifflin, 1974.

Konvitz, Milton R. *Bill of Rights Reader*. 5th ed. Ithaca, N.Y.: Cornell Univ. Press, 1973.

La Morte, Michael W., Harold W. Gentry and D. Parker Young. *Students' Legal Rights and Responsibilities*. Cincinatti: W.H. Anderson Co., 1971.

Langton, Kenneth P. *Political Socialization*. New York: Oxford Univ. Press, 1969.

Levine, Alan H. *The Rights of Students*. An American Civil Liberties Union Handbook. New York: E.P. Dutton & Co., 1973.

Lines, P.M., ed. *The Constitutional Rights of Students*. Cambridge, Mass.: Harvard Center for Law and Education, 1976.

Maguire, Frederick W. and Richard M. Spong. *Journalism and the Student Publication*. New York: McGraw Hill, 1951.

Meissner, William W. *The Assault on Authority*. Maryknoll, N.Y.: Orbis Books, 1971

Nelson, Jack, ed. *Captive Voices: High School Journalism in America*. The Report of the Commission of Inquiry into High School Journalism. New York: Schocken Books, 1974.

Nielson, H. Dean. *Tolerating Political Dissent*. International Association for the Evaluation of Educational Achievement, Monograph Studies No. 6. Stockholm, Sweden: Almqvist & Wiksell International, 1977.

Prosser William L. *Handbook of the Law of Torts*. 4th ed. St. Paul, Minn.: West Publishing Co., 1971.

Remmers, H.H., ed. *Anti-Democratic Attitudes in American Schools*. Evanston, Ill.: Northwestern Univ. Press, 1963.

Reutter, E. Edmund, Jr. *Legal Aspects of Control of Student Activities by Public School Authorities.* Washington, D.C.: National Organization on Legal Problems of Education, 1970.

Rhodes, Clifford, ed. *Authority in a Changing Society.* London: Constable & Co., 1969.

Sennett, Richard. *Authority.* New York: Alfred A. Knopf, 1980.

Simon, Yves R. *A General Theory of Authority.* Notre Dame, Ind.: Univ. of Notre Dame Press, 1962

Stevens, George E. and John B. Webster. *Law and the Student Press.* Ames, Iowa: Iowa State Univ. Press, 1973.

Tice, Terrence N. *Student Rights, Decisionmaking, and the Law.* ERIC/Higher Education Report No. 10. Washington D.C.: American Association for Higher Education, 1976.

Tribe, Laurence H. *American Constitutional Law.* Mineola, N.Y.: Foundation Press, 1978.

White, Graham. *Socialisation.* London: Longman, 1977.

Williamson, E.G. and John L. Cowan. *The American Students' Freedom of Expression.* Minneapolis: Univ. of Minnesota Press, 1966.

Woods, L.B. *A Decade of Censorship in America.* Metuchen, N.J.: Scarecrow Press, 1979.

Wrightsman, Lawrence S. *Social Psychology.* 2nd ed. Monterey, Calif.: Brooks/Cole Publishing Co., 1977.

Zeigler, Carol L. *Struggle in the Schools: Constitutional Protections for Public High School Students.* Princeton University: Woodrow Wilson Association Monograph Series in Public Affairs No. 1, 1970.